Author Masterminds

An Anthology: Collection of a Clutch of Creative,
Canny, and Compelling Authors

Carl Douglass, Mary Flint, Adam Freestone, Walter Grant,
Cil Gregoire, Victoria Hardesty, Steve Levi, Gordon Parker,
Irene Pettice, Mary Ann Poll, James Qeqe, Rich Ritter,
Magdel Roets, Evan Swensen, Rebecca Wetzler, and Valerie Winans

PUBLICATION
CONSULTANTS
We Believe In The Power Of Authors

PO Box 221974 Anchorage, Alaska 99522-1974
books@publicationconsultants.com—www.publicationconsultants.com

ISBN Number: 978-1-59433-912-7
eBook ISBN Number: 978-1-59433-913-4

Copyright 2019 Publication Consultants
—First Edition—

Manufactured in the United States of America

Contents

A Feather in Your Heart

Mary Flint
America's Most Promising Science Fiction Writer

Based on a Japanese folktale called "Tsuru no Ongaeshi"
(Crane's Return of a Favor) or "Tsuru Nyobo" (Crane Wife).

The only sound was that of the shuttle on my loom going back and forth, weaving the delicate threads. My back and knees ached from staying in the same position for hours, and my hands shook from fatigue. An awful fit of coughing echoed through the tiny house, and I glanced nervously behind me, but the door was still shut, just as

I had left it. I paused my weaving for a moment and adjusted my shawl around my shivering shoulders. Autumn days would turn to winter soon, and already the cold northern winds were blowing and finding all the tiny holes in this drafty house.

"You deserve better than a drafty house on a lonely farm." I remembered my husband saying those words to me one cold winter day. He had built a large fire in the fireplace, but it hadn't seemed to help much against the cold. We had sat together in front of the fire with hot tea.

I had shrugged after he had said those words. "But I'm happy in this drafty house," I had replied, "and I don't think this farm is lonely."

He had smiled, too. "If you say so," he'd whispered, kissing my forehead.

Then he had told me a story he had told every winter since we had met. He told me how one day, as he had been traveling back to his farm from gathering firewood, he had stumbled across a crane. The magnificent creature had gotten its leg stuck in a hunter's trap; its head drooped in defeat. Dropping his load, my husband had rushed to free the bird, which, thankfully, had been uninjured.

"I'll never forget how beautiful that crane was, as it flew away that day," he would say to finish his tale.

I smiled at the memory now. That winter seemed like only yesterday, even though it had been three winters ago. My smile faded as I heard another fit of coughing, this one lasted longer than the first. I had to hurry.

I returned to my weaving; forcing my tired, sore fingers to work even faster. The shuttle moved back and forth, back and forth, adding rows to the fabric. I had always received compliments for my weaving. The colors were vibrant, and my finished fabrics had been praised as better than the finest silks.

At first, I had only made one bolt. It had been my second autumn with my husband. A falling tree in a windstorm had damaged our house, and drought had been heavy that year. The crops had died, leaving us with nothing to sell in exchange for the things we needed to survive the winter. We had only had a little food, and since the crops had died, no seed to plant the next spring. We had no friends or family to help us, and I could tell that my husband was worried. So I had offered to weave something to sell. My only condition was that he never watch me weave. This request had puzzled him, but he had accepted. He had kept his promise as I wove a bolt of cloth over the next few days.

I had sold the cloth to a passing nobleman when we had visited a nearby village. It was he who had given my cloth such high praise, declaring it finer than any of the foreign silks he had ever seen. He had paid us enough to repair our house and buy and preserve food and seeds for next spring.

The same nobleman had offered to buy more cloth from me the next time we visited the village, but I had kindly refused. My husband had never asked me to weave any more, he merely asked from time to time where I had learned to weave such fine cloth. I always replied, "I taught myself," which wasn't a lie, I *had* taught myself how to weave, but really, it was the material that made the difference.

I thought that would be the only time I wove such cloth, and for a while, it had been. Until last summer.

We had been tending to our crops since sunup, as usual, but my husband had fallen ill very suddenly, collapsing in the field. I had scraped together enough money for a doctor, but he had only brought bad news. There was medicine for my husband's condition, but it had to be imported from another continent. There was no way we could possibly afford it ...

Unless I wove my cloth again.

And so I had returned to my loom, working as fast as I could. One bolt, then two. I sold them both, and then learned that the roads had flooded, I would have to pay extra to have the medicine delivered all the way to the village. I wove two more bolts and sold them, too. Then, I learned that there had been a storm at sea, and several vials of the medicine had broken. There was a limited supply left. I would have to pay even more if I wanted any.

One more bolt would have to be enough. I wouldn't be able to weave any more after that.

The shuttle moved back and forth, the thread cutting into my fingers, making them bleed. My shoulders cramped and my neck ached. The sun went down and the wind blew harder as I shivered. The coughing from the other room increased, and fear clenched my heart.

This bolt has to be enough, I thought urgently.

Then I stopped, just one row short of a finished piece of cloth. Just one more row, and I could buy the medicine, right? But that meant ...

I took a deep breath and checked behind me one more time, ensuring that the door was still closed. Not that there was much to be worried about. My husband was too weak to sit up. There was no way he could come in.

I stared at the feather I held in my hand. My last feather. I had plucked it from my wing. For the crane my husband had rescued, all those winters ago, had been me. Moved so much by his kindness, I had transformed myself into a human, so that I might repay him in some way. I had never expected him to fall in love with me, nor I with him, but Fate has a funny way of giving us exactly what we need when we least expect it. Never had I been so happy as I had been living here, but my husband did not know the truth. How could he? Whatever would he think of me?

But as I moved to slide the feather into the shuttle, enough to finish the cloth, I hesitated. For there was a chance, once I had finished weaving this cloth, when the feather was gone, I would remain a crane for the rest of my days. A tear slipped down my face as I stared at the feather.

"But will he still love me," I whispered, "if I must remain a crane?"

I felt arms wrap around me, as my husband's large hand held mine, closing the feather into my fingers.

"I knew all along, my dear," he said kindly. "Only you could be as beautiful as that crane!"

I turned to look at him in surprise, and he gently brushed a tear from my face. "I've known all along how you've lost your wings for me," he continued, "something I could never hope to repay you for."

Then he gently kissed the feather I held in my hand. "But I promise, my dear, I'll love you always, with your feather in my heart."

April Showers Bring May Flowers

Nancy Perez
Author of Action, Adventure and Suspense with Arabian Horses

April showers bring May flowers; at least that's what my Grandparents used to tell me. I have often counted on those showers to give my landscaping a boost. Years ago when I subscribed to the belief that I was super woman I owned a fairly large yard. The lawn did well everywhere except under the black walnut tree that had matured decades before I became steward of the property. All parts of the walnut tree contain a toxin which inhibits the growth of nearby plants. The roots contain that toxin also so growth can be affected for several feet from the perimeter of the tree. I didn't know that at that time. But, I had a deep-seated sense of optimism.

"If I could dream it, I could make it happen" was my motto. My family had been farmers and taught me many things about planting and growing. My dream was to have an English cottage garden, unstructured and profuse with carnations, hollyhocks, sweet Williams and lavender. I could see myself settled in a garden lounge, under my walnut tree, breathing in the scents of the flowers. I would have a cup of tea, delicate bone china of course and a book, a classic to go with the romance of the scene. It never entered my mind that I had never seen a walnut tree in the farming community I grew up in. Not recognizing the significance of that was a mistake. My next mistake was planning my dream garden.

Planning included preparing the ground and buying plants. Still armed with the "I can make it happen" attitude I hauled in topsoil, turned and conditioned the earth. The need for the feeling of accomplishment was so great I did it all myself with shovel, gloves and rubber boots. This is back breaking work but no helpful gardeners for this determined lady. Of course I didn't want to wait too long to see the fruits of my labor so I bought mature plants and plenty of them just in case. It took several weekends and evenings after work to go from planning to finished garden. I was so tired and sore I couldn't appreciate what I had accomplished. "Next weekend", I told myself.

It actually took a few weeks for everything to be just right. Then I made my third mistake. I invited the wrong cousin over for tea in my new garden.

My cousin was an accomplished gardener herself and I secretly wanted to show her up just a little. All right, more than a little. It would be a rite of passage, "see cuz I can do something just as artistic as you can, naner, naner." In my dream, she walks up my pathway exclaiming proudly how beautiful the garden turned out. She compliments me on my choice of plants and the inspired layout of the various types. The syrupy compliments pour from her mouth. As she walks in my front door my dream floats off like a puffy cloud and I come back down to Earth with the thump of the screen door closing. What did she just say?

"Plants will not survive under a black walnut tree, the juglone toxin is in all parts of the tree and will cause your plants to yellow, wilt and eventually die. The root system can extend three to four times the diameter of the canopy of the tree so I'm surprised your lawn is still surviving."

"Oh, you spoilsport, smarty-pants" is what went through my mind. The words stayed in my head and didn't come spilling out of my mouth but my disappointment was profound. I wanted this garden for a long time and so much work went into it. What hurt the most was hoping for acceptance from my most admired cousin. I had always felt lacking in comparison to this cousin. She was so talented and beautiful. I wanted her to express approval of me.

She was right though. The garden did not survive. Year in and year out I tried different plants, supplements and techniques and eventually everything turned yellow, wilted and died. You see, the fact that very few plants will thrive under a walnut tree was just too simple. What I believed and acted on was that my cousin didn't approve of me. Therefore something was lacking in me and I couldn't get my garden to grow. Putting it that simply seems absolutely absurd in the light of many years of maturing.

Now Dear Reader, do not think that I spent agonized years of sorrow because I couldn't get my cousin to love me and to get my garden to grow. Eventually I got the gardening fever out of my system and enjoyed every year of try and fail and try again. Now I have a postage stamp sized yard, just big enough for a couple hearty rose bushes and my lounge chair. The book and the tea service still accompany my idyllic Saturday afternoons.

That cousin shuns the entire family now. It sounds like something deeper was at the heart of our strained tea party but why go there? My garden projects were never very special but in some ways they always were a success. They say it is the journey that counts for more than the destination.

Again, I must say it seems absolutely absurd that we humans need to fail numerous times to learn a simple lesson. Or maybe it is absurd that I have a hard time accepting that is just the way we are.

If you are like me, you are wondering how that fateful tea party ended up. This is what my memory has archived: we ate and chatted and drank tea. We laughed and gossiped and drank more tea. At sunset I carried the tea tray in to the house and my cousin gathered her purse and jacket and started down my long path. She appeared as relieved as I the day had come to an end. Just as she stepped under the mighty black walnut tree the heavens opened up. I've never experienced such a torrential April shower. The remaining sunlight glinted off the leaves and the raindrops splashed the black soot from the tree and deposited it all over my dear cousin.

The following month is the only month I did have glorious May flowers. And my cousin never got the spots out of her dress.

A Sled Dog

by Remington Beagle
as told to
Valerie Winans
Dog's Best Friend

It was cold even by Nome standards, and I was curled up in my doghouse preserving energy. I heard the other dogs before I saw Kaasen. There was a true husky cacophony as he began to hitch dogs to the gang line. "Pick me! Pick me!" they were all shouting. He hooked up Moctoc, Slim, Billy, Tilly, Sye, and Fox. I was surprised when he hooked up Fox behind the lead position. Who would he put in lead? Yikes! It's me.

Off we went into the night in a blizzard with a wind chill of 70 below. The wind was whipping the snow so bad it was impossible to see very far or for very long. Smell and touch were senses I needed the most in this situation, and as I concentrated on using my smell and touch to the utmost I was also focused on pulling and staying on the trail. Kaasen put his trust in me, and I put all of my trust in him. I knew when he pulled me out for the lead position in Nome it would be a challenge. This is just what I was waiting for. I knew Seppala thought of me as second rate, and I needed the chance to prove him wrong.

The trip from Nome to Bluff was uneventful, and after we got to Bluff it was a waiting game. We were fed and rested when Olson pulled in, and it was our turn to make a run. I was anxious to get started, as was the rest of the team. Dogs sense a lot, and we all sensed the importance of this run. The wind had scoured the trail bare in some spots, but then suddenly there was a huge drift. I tried to run through it and got stuck. I struggled inside the drift to move, but soon realized it was futile.

I could hear and feel Kaasen floundering through the snowdrift toward me. He was a big guy and moved a lot of snow around to free us from this mess. He grabbed my harness and turned me and the whole team behind me around to go back the way we had come. When we were steered the other way around the ridge I knew what my job was. Nose to the ground we edged around the ridge while I frantically searched for the smell or the feel of the trail. We absolutely had to regain the trail.

Just as I was about to give up hope and stop I got a faint smell of canine. One more leap ahead and yes—here's the trail. I found it! My joy at finding the trail again was felt all down the line, and my team lunged with me to full momentum.

Dogs are pack animals by nature. I guess it comes from our ancestors the wolves. Packs will pick their own natural leaders—the alpha dog if you will. I was not picked by the pack. Gunnar Kaasen picked me, and I had to prove myself to my teammates as well as Kaasen. If the team did not accept me as leader there would be dissension, and other dogs along the line would try to assert their authority. That would be bad. The trail we were on was perilous, and the weather was worse. Dissension could mean death for all of us.

Soon I became aware we were on a river. The surface was pure ice. Oh, no! I could see and feel that my feet were wet. Water on top of ice is never a good thing. I stopped right there. I looked back at Kaasen for direction. He came to the head of the team and could see a very large overflow in front of us. I got a, "Good dog! Good dog!" Kaasen guided us to go "gee" and off of the river. When we were safely off of the river, he approached each of us with a pet, dry booties, and salmon snack. This action helped to secure team confidence in me.

As I led my team up the snow covered mountain, I had to keep my head down because the wind was blowing tiny ice daggers in my face. I relied on my sense of smell and the feel of the ground under my booted paws to keep me from leading the team, myself, and Klaasen over the edge of the ridge.

Although I couldn't see it I knew that to our "haw" was a fall of many feet to the beach below. The wind gusts whipped the sled from side to side making it nearly impossible to stay on the narrow trail that led the way up Topkok Mountain. The wheel dogs at the back of the pack nearest the sled took the brunt of the punishment from the wind as it jerked them one way and then the other.

We reached the top, raced down the icy slope, and then we had more frozen water to cross. The snow was being blown so hard that we often had to go only by smell and feel once again. Not an easy thing to do at our pace of even 5 or 6 miles per hour. I was not getting much direction from Kaasen; he had turned the team over to me. I knew I had to keep pulling and keep on the trail. I hardly felt the cold and ice—I was totally focused on moving ahead.

When the sled flipped over in the wind, and slid into a snow bank we were all yanked back to a full stop. I looked back for Kaasen, but he was nowhere in sight. Where in the world was he? I saw the snow flying up out of the drift before I saw him struggling out.

Next thing I saw was him charging back into the snow drift, and I thought he had lost his mind. But when he emerged again he was carrying the precious package, which was our responsibility to deliver. Thank goodness! It was a miracle he could find it in the middle of a snowdrift in the middle of a blizzard. Dogs know God and His providence. Dog is God spelled backwards after all.

We got back on the trail, and the trail and weather seemed to improve a little. I was encouraged we would make our destination after all.

As we neared Port Safety we could see everything was dark. We paused there momentarily, but then pushed on. There would be no stop for us at Port Safety. Running next to the beach we continually had to charge through snowdrifts. Sometimes Kaasen would go ahead and stomp down the snow ahead of us.

I was exhausted and feeling stiffer by each step, and my team was tired and stiff as well. I knew as lead dog if I faltered at all it would be a signal to others it was okay to stop. I kept repeating to myself, "just keep going, just keep going," and somehow we did.

When I was about to lose hope again I saw a light ahead giving me hope because it looked like the light I had seen on other trips signaling the end of the trail at Nome. It was the lighted cross on top of St. Joseph's Church.

Sure enough we were soon on the streets of Nome, but strangely there were no people in sight. Kaasen reined us in to a stop, came to the front of the line, hugged me up tight to and said, "You are a fine dog." All the thanks I needed. My heart was full from the love and appreciation of Kaasen, and the acceptance of the team.

In the distance I heard voices. It sounded like, "Remington, Remington Beagle, wake up! I thought, "My name isn't Remington—it's Balto." Then someone was ruffing my ears and scratching my back.

As I open my eyes there I was curled up on the couch, and Val was trying to wake me up. I just had the most amazing dream!

Did you ever have a dream so real it stays with you after you are awake? This one will be with me for days to come for sure. I just love being a hero.

Be Specific

Magdel Roets
Writer of Christian Fiction

Some people say when you need something, ask. God will provide and you must be satisfied with whatever He gives. Others would tell you to ask God for what you need, but you must be specific.

Tell God exactly what it is you want. Don't say: "God, I need a car. Please give me a car." Rather say: "God, I need a brand new cherry red Carrera 911 with barley coloured interior," or "God I want a twenty year old four-by-four pickup double cab, sky-blue with a white canopy and tan interior, tinted windows and a tow-bar."

Perhaps it works that way. I don't know; haven't tried it—yet. May be I should. After a friend told me the following story, I was half-convinced.

My friend, let's call her Emmie, was standing in the order queue at the newly opened branch of KFC franchise in her local shopping centre three weeks before. The queue was long, but everyone was longsuffering because it was the weekly payday for the workers and a KFC meal was a payday treat for many.

Now, as things go, there is always something, or someone to test one's patience. That day it was a man. From the odour, and rags he wore he was obviously homeless. This guy was hanging around close by the KFC order queue.

Some people were nervous, watching his every movement. He was either fiddling with his cuffs, scratching his scalp while leaning on the bordering railing. Every few seconds he shifted his weight from one leg to the other and glared at the people waiting to place their order. Every so often he left his post, strolled away just to return a few seconds later.

Emmie felt quite a bit uneasy when she caught him openly assessing her appearance. She clutched her bag tightly under her arm praying the queue would move faster. Slowly the queue was getting shorter as orders were placed and the hungry moved over to the queue where they waited next to the dispatch counter.

Not deliberately did she listen to the others but could not help overhearing what the woman behind her was saying: "Not long to wait now, Sweet Pie. Just hold my hand and stay close to me. That uncle is watching."

Another commented mumbling: "He's not watching the child. He's watching our wallets." Everyone who heard this clutched their bags or purses even tighter. The men checked their pockets to make sure their wallets were still in there.

Emmie's queue moved up until there was only one person in front of her. Suddenly the homeless man staggered closer swayed and fell down at Emmie's feet, clasping his stomach, eyes rolling and moaning softly. The atmosphere changed and everybody crowded the fallen in shock and sympathy. Guilt played a roll. They all were about to have a feast and here is this poor guy fainted from hunger. Right in front of their eyes.

One of the shop assistants brought a wet cloth to dab his face. Another tried to help him sit up. He was still groaning when someone produced an apple from a bag and offered it to him. "Here, Sir, have this apple. It is not much, but it might get you past the worst hunger."

Before she finished her last sentence, the man rose, miraculously revived, jumped to his feet and indignantly replied: "Madam, if I wanted an apple I would have gone fainting in front of Fruit-'n-Veg."

Emmie told me after a stunned silence the crowd started laughing. They all pitched in and bought the homeless man exactly the KFC meal he wanted. He was very specific when he placed his order and went to the right place to do his fainting. However, I doubt it would produce the same result in front of the Porsche dealer.

Broken Vessels

James Qeqe
The New Voice of Africa

In life, there are two things I can never explain. That a man cried for help to my ears and I did not hear, and that very same man disappeared as nothing that existed. Everyone needs a friend, or someone very close to his or her heart. But once one has that, people always question, 'what is happening between those two?' But one thing they'll never do is to ask one of you.

The vessels are broken, the heart is torn apart. Four years ago, when the vessels were made, everything seemed to be perfect. No one questioned. Four years down the line all vanished. The vessels are broken. Only if we would see the future, we would actually be different. Anyway, we can still see what is to come, by learning from other people's experiences. Hence I am sharing this with you today. If I have learnt anything in this life, only this, that there are two types of pain in life, the pain that hurts you, and the pain that changes you.

The fact is, in life we all going to lose someone we love in one way or the other. If you haven't, count yourself blessed, which I doubt if none hasn't. Come on! It's 2019.

It is not easy to distinguish difference between the pain that hurts and that which changes you, hence you need time to see through it. It is very hard to answer the question 'what's wrong?' when there's nothing right.

You can see many smiles in the world, BUT you can never know whose world is upside down. In my ears, I can still hear his cries, but I cannot do anything now, it's finished. I can never be the same—never. Everyone in this world can be your friend, but not everyone in this world can be an ear to your cries. And that's the honest truth, which I will never compromise on. That was the man who cried to my ears, whom I did not hear. That was a friend, a brother, and an angel. But I failed. And it's not just a failure; I failed dismally.

Only if we could rewind the time like a movie we would all right our individual wrongs. To make them better, to make others smile too, as we once smiled. To see the best in others, as some saw best in us as well. To make life easier for others, as we were taken care of at some point. When the vessels are broken, everything becomes miserable, why? Because without the vessels you cannot contain anything. Let alone the precious vessel that only contains the precious gifts and them alone. Not every vessel is the same, every vessel has its own tilos that is to say: its own purpose. You can never replace any vessel with anything. Same as to people, you can never replace anyone with anyone and with anything. Not even money can do that, not even gold can. I wish to share this with you that take every person you meet as a vessel that will never be replace, before that vessel be broken and irreplaceable.

I read somewhere, in 2015 that: "It's not because you don't care, but because they don't care."

I still find myself feeling sad. No one can handle your heart better than you, so don't give it to a person and then complain. Well what if you're too late? What if you have given it to someone already? Well, it's not too late, do not reclaim it but make it a point that you own a good fortune of it. Have a room for disappointments, make sure that room is empty and beautiful, and make sure that it is clean, so that when you get disappointed, you would silently visit it, without first needing to clean or remove some stuff out of it.

In life, there are mornings that you would have to say to your pillow, "Dear Pillow, sorry for all the tears that I shared last night... I could not help it, it was heavy for me... besides, tonight is not guaranteed that it won't happen again. Please Pillow, have a space for my emotions too."

Look, it's very easy to hurt someone and then just say sorry again. But believe me, it's very difficult to get hurt and then say "I'm fine!"

I once experienced this, someone asked me what was wrong, and I smiled and said nothing. When they turned around and a tear came down and I whispered to myself... *Everything is* and if you want to know what's that... it's a broken vessel.

In a way I am proud of my heart, it's been played, cheated, stabbed and even broken like a vessel, but somehow, it still works, it still love, it still cares. Have you ever listened to a song, and you start crying out of nowhere? Let me tell you something. Most of the times, it's not the song that makes you cry or emotional, but it's the people and things that come to mind when you hear it. The worst battle is the one that goes on between your heart and your mind. Because you just never know which one to listen to.

Every heart has a pain. Only the way of expressing it is different. Fools hide it in eyes while the wise hide it in their smile. So never try to hide your secrets and emotions from someone who can read your eyes. Because often those who can read our eyes are experts in reading our heart. Some pretend to be caring, and actually would even appear as people who care, but deep down their hearts they don't, they only want what could be the topic for the news head-lines. We have people like that; we have friends like that. I would prefer physical pain than emotional pain. Because physical pain can heal, but emotional pain will always be there.

It's also very easy to say "busy" when someone needs you, but trust me, it's very hard to hear "busy" when you need someone.

Let's try again. Distance is not an obstacle but space not filled. Sometimes I wish I were a little kid again. Skinned knees are easier to fix than broken vessels.

I hope you get the message.

Dad Was A Democrat

Irene Petteice
Senior Author of Political Perspectives
Author Masterminds Charter Member

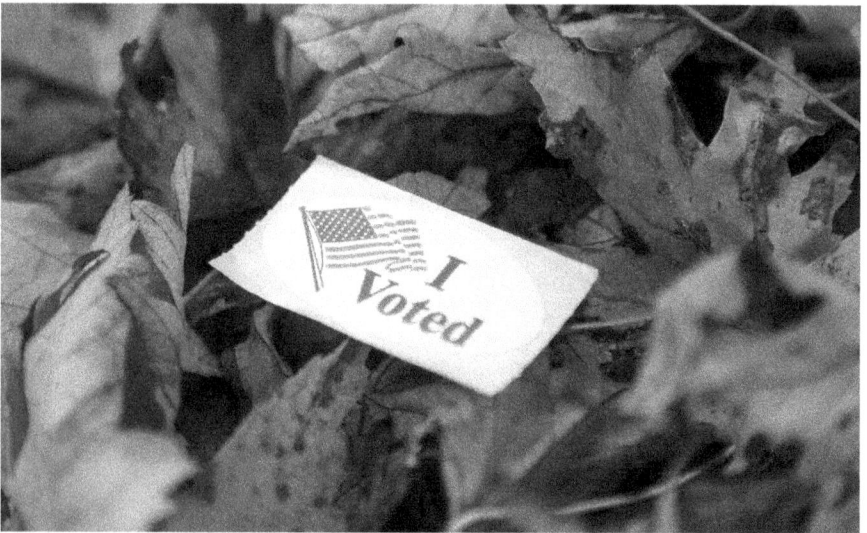

In 1961, I applied for a position as a court reporter for the Coroner's Office.

The Coroner is an elected official, and my boss was a Republican. He was not just a Coroner. He was an ordained minister, a family man with grown children of his own, and later I found out he knew my father.

Now whether that had to do with anything or not, I don't know. I prefer to believe I had my own talents and abilities.

My main job in the office was to sit in the office all day and answer the phone (which almost never rang), and when we had an inquest since I was very fast with shorthand and typing, it was my job to write down everything everyone said and then later type it up. Most of my livelihood was made up of what money I received from the transcripts of the Inquests that were purchased by different lawyers, because the meager salary paid by the Coroner's Office was less than $2,700 per year.

I do know that my boss felt fatherly toward me and watched over me. One day he asked me to drive him out on a call. Another time we went to a funeral home to see a body and talk to the mortician who had already begun the embalming process. They kept asking me if I was okay. He respected the fact that I did not faint or become ill at the sight of blood or a dead body and soon started asking me to drive him on most calls.

For anyone that has read my book *You Never Die*, you already have the answer to that, but I did not disclose the reason to my boss.

My boss told me he had cataracts in his eyes, so he made me a deputy and allowed me to chauffeur him on calls and out-of-town inquests.

When I became engaged to be married, my boss married my future husband and I. Since my husband worked out of the city and was only home on weekends, the County Clerk came to my apartment on Saturday afternoon and issued our marriage license.

When you work for an elected official, you are told you must donate to the Party every year, whether you want to or can afford to or not. The Party told me I had to pay $100. That was a lot of money for me. A month's rent in those days was only $30.

If you vote in the primary election, you must vote a straight Republican or Democratic ticket. To void this, you wait until the General Election, and you can vote for anyone you wish.

The Election Bureau was across the hall from my office in the courthouse. There was never a shortage of republican and democratic bumper stickers.

Now, my father, on the other hand, was a Democrat. For as long as I can remember, Dad was a Democrat.

Whenever there was an election coming up Dad listened to every speech on the radio. I don't think he ever missed listening to Walter Cronkite or Chet Huntley and David Brinkley. When I was very little we had a radio that you hooked up to a car battery and on Saturday night after the news we listened to *The Creaking Door*, *Fibber McGee and Molly*, and then Minnie Pearl would come out yelling, "Howdy, I'm just so glad to see you," and you knew it was time for the *Grand Ole Opry*.

I never figured there was anything good about the platform of a Democrat, but Dad worked for the State, and everyone knows that Illinois is full of Democrats.

Dad wasn't much of one for teasing, so I never said anything to him about being a Democrat – well that is until I left home.

I lived in an apartment next door to a grocery store, and he and my mother would shop there on Saturday morning. My little brother would come over while they shopped, and then they would stop to visit awhile.

One Saturday morning, my brother and I took a bunch of Republican bumper stickers out to the parking lot and stuck them to Dad's front and rear car bumpers.

When Mom and Dad finished shopping and came to my apartment, Dad didn't say anything at all, but he had a gleam in his eye.

Now, Mom claimed to be an Independent and always said she and Dad canceled out each other's votes. My sister never paid attention to who was running or what they stood for. She was a died-in-the-wool Democrat because she worked in the election office on the day of the election, and the Democrats paid her $100 to work all day and handed her a Democrat ballot to vote.

How I got involved in politics, I am not certain. I think it is because of the fact that my brother gave 20 years of his life for this country that I became a patriot. He was in the Army and in missiles and hated the idea of killing so many people, and when he was in Desert Storm, and I was at work, and the television was on, and that first missile went off, I went outside and cried like a baby.

Since that time, I have been a political activist. I am 78 years of age. I have worked steadily since I left high school. When I went to college, it was at night after I put in a full day's work. In all my years, I never drew one unemployment check from our government. I am still working by choice because I like writing; it keeps my mind active.

But I am tired. I am tired of all those young people that don't have a work ethic. I am tired of their parents that have not taught them what it means to have a work ethic and what satisfaction they can receive from a job well done.

I am tired of living with the generation of children raised by parents that, instead of preparing them for adulthood, shifting instead to the elusive goal of feeling good, trying is as good as achieving and that all ideas were equal. There is no more individual study, stars or trophies, no winning or losing, no reason for goal setting. The problem is this; adults now do not have coping skills.

I am tired of all of the liberals that are now telling me that I have to spread the wealth. I am tired of the government telling me I have to spend so much of my retirement money every year so they can tax it.

I'm tired of being told I must lower my living standard to fight global warming when the ones fighting on behalf of global warming are getting rich.

Right now, I'm sick and tired of the Democrats blaming all of their mistakes on our President. I'm tired of all the lies. I am not worn-out tired. I am fight-back tired.

Dad is gone now. The Democrats have moved a long way since his day. They have a new name or them now - Socialist Democrat.

Am I Republican? I consider myself an Independent because I will take the time to listen and research a candidate to see what he stands for before I decide to vote.

Too many people are unaware that Progressive, Socialist, Marxist, and Communist are all the same thing. Some of the older generations remember when members of Hollywood were black-balled from working for being Communists.

Now we have more than eighty elected Congressmen working in our Capitol that are members of the Communist Party of America. Where is the public outrage?

The only Democrat I ever voted for was John F. Kennedy. That was while I was working for a Republican. I wondered at the time if I did the right thing. I must have. The Democrats apparently didn't like him.

December Bear

Robin Barefield
Alaska Wilderness Mystery Author

December is a tricky time of year on Kodiak Island. The temperature can hover in the forties, winds calm, and the sky clear, but an hour later, it might drop to twenty degrees with fifty mph winds, snow blowing sideways, and no visibility. A quick flight to town by floatplane can turn into a weeklong ordeal while waiting for the weather to improve enough to fly home.

One year in early December, my husband, Mike, chartered a floatplane for the forty-five-minute flight from our remote lodge to the town of Kodiak. Calm winds and cloudless skies provided easy plane travel. Our deer hunts had recently ended, and deer meat hung in the meat shed. Mike planned to fly to town, run his errands, and fly home the next day to process the meat. Clear weather brings freezing nighttime temperatures, so the meat in the shed was frozen solid, and we didn't worry about it attracting bears. Mike's trip to town turned out to be longer than expected, though, when a low-pressure system sped over the island, and a storm hit the following day. One night turned into two and then three.

I stayed by myself at the lodge, but I wasn't worried; the generator and oil heater purred without a hitch. My routine was to turn on the generator in the evening and then turn it off again just before I went to bed. The only inconvenience was I had to walk 100 feet (30.5 m) to the generator shed. The straightest path from the house to the shed is down a wooden walk, but ice covered the walk, making it nearly impassable. Instead, I took the longer, safer route behind the house, past the meat shed, and between our two guest cabins.

My third evening alone at the lodge, the temperature soared above freezing, and to my delight, the ice on the walk began to melt. It didn't at first occur to me that this rise in the mercury meant the deer meat was also thawing. At bedtime, I grabbed my flashlight for my nightly trek to the generator shed. I started to head up the trail past the meat shed, but at the last moment, I realized the ice had melted from the walk, so I took the more direct route. Once I returned to the house, I bolted the door and got ready for bed in the pitch-dark house. Just as I was sliding under the covers, I heard the unmistakable noise of something ripping boards from the side of a building, and the ripping sounds emanated from the direction of the meat shed. I considered my options briefly but quickly decided I did not want to confront a bear on a dark, moonless night, so I crawled into bed and pulled the covers over my head, somehow managing to fall asleep.

The next morning, I thought I'd imagined the late-night commotion. The shed appeared fine when I looked at it through the kitchen window, but then I saw a fox on the hill behind the shed and then another fox and then three eagles, all eating something. I hurried outdoors and down the walk to get a view of the shed from a different angle, and sure enough, the bear had removed most of the rear wall, pulled the deer meat outside, enjoyed a feast, and graciously left the scraps for the other forest creatures. I didn't see the bear, but I knew he probably hadn't gone far, and as soon as he digested his repast from the previous evening, he'd return in search of his next meal. I called Mike and reported the situation, and he told me to be careful and said he'd be home as soon as the weather improved.

The skies briefly cleared in Kodiak, and it looked as if Mike might get home soon to help me with my bear situation, but as I waited for the plane, the snow began to fall. Pilots flying around the rugged, mountainous terrain of Kodiak Island must be able to see where they are flying, and heavy snow destroys visibility. I stared out the window as the snow showers continued. At times the snow slowed, but at others, the mountains disappeared in a swirl of white. I called the airlines and reported our weather, and the pilot decided to delay the flight. I wanted Mike to get home and help me with the bear, but I did not want him to fly in poor weather. As I waited, my anxiety built, and when I received a VHF radio call from a nearby deer hunter saying a plane had crashed in the bay, and he was bringing the pilot to our lodge, I feared Mike was on the downed plane. As it turned out, though, a wheel plane plowed into the water in heavy snow. The pilot appeared cold, wet, and shaken, and the aircraft was destroyed, but miraculously, the plane carried no passengers, and the pilot wasn't hurt.

Mike finally flew home later the same afternoon, and the pilot from the crash jumped on the plane for the flight back to town. We removed the remaining deer meat from the shed and processed it, and then we repaired the damaged shed. Once we emptied the shed of food, the bear had no reason to stay, and he went on his way.

I have always wondered what would have happened that night if I'd chosen to walk down the trail past the meat shed after I turned off the generator. I likely would have collided with a hungry bear intent on locating the deer meat he could smell. Maybe he would have run from me, and then again, maybe not. I decided I would not spend another December night alone in the wilderness.

Do You Think I'm Crazy?

Walter Grant
One of America's Enduring Patriot Authors

Prologue

Between struggling with writing and surviving daily challenges, referenced by some as life, there are times when I'm lost between fantasy and reality. Perhaps I live in the abyss separating the two, continually oscillating between the netherworld and the only universe most others know or consider. Is there a difference—are they one and the same?

Questions must be asked: how do we know what we know, what do we see while not looking, what do we hear when not listening? Is it insane to acknowledge the possibility that not all data stored in the ferrite cores of our minds has been collected from experiences in the world we wake up in every day? Do we always wake up in the same world? Would our body sensors know the difference?

If one gave such queries more than a fleeting second would their sanity be called into question? Is insanity unique to only the creatures we are—humans?

This demands another question: are dreams fragments of the past or a glimpse into the future? Who's past? Who's future?

Is life, as we know it, a game structured by a superhuman race for their own pleasure? Are we programmed?

For whom do you play? Who is your gamemaster? What game piece are you?

" . . . Knowing is not enough . . . ." Leonardo da Vinci

"Honey, who was on the phone?"

"Louise, she invited us to dinner. I accepted."

Jack and Louise were good people. The kind of folks you want as neighbors. They were always there for their friends and never asked anything in return. Jack and I had been friends since childhood and I had no reason to believe that would ever change; however, I didn't like eating dinner at their house. Louise was a great cook, and it showed—she carried an extra eighty pounds on her five-foot, two-inch frame.

I liked her cooking. The problem for me: she insisted everyone have second servings. She appeared dejected whenever I declined. So, as to not hurt her feelings, I always ate more than I wanted and, unquestionably, more than I should. By taking small first portions, I was able to take even less when I selected second helpings and not feel uncomfortable at the end of the meal, although I always made a big deal about being stuffed. Even after eating small portions I'd diet for two or three days after every meal we ate at her house.

Unlike me, Sandy, my lovely wife, never refused second and third helpings, especially desserts. She didn't appear to be aware that her dress size had more than quadrupled since we married—to be kind, I'll say she pushed the scales several pounds past pleasingly plump. Everyone knew I didn't eat sweets; by using high blood sugar as an excuse, I was able to refuse the desserts Louise so proudly served—such as buttery opened-faced fruit tortes on puff paste, crème brûlée, and soufflés with crème fraîche. I would sip café noir while discussing things of little or no importance and watch the others consume five or six thousand calories they didn't need and shouldn't eat. I couldn't figure out how Jack kept so trim. He stood an even six feet and weighed 170 pounds—two inches taller than me, but only ten pounds heavier.

Sandy and Louise arranged bowls with generous servings of apple and cherry torte covered with Chantilly Crème alongside linen napkins and silverware on a serving tray. They added Riesling glasses containing what remained of the dessert wine from dinner—a trockenbeerenauslese. Satisfied with their selections, they picked up the thousand calorie trays and retired to the media room to discuss children and grandkids while watching Secret Garden or some other old movie with a love-story ending.

Jack and I cloistered in the library with snifters of Remy Martin X.O. Excellence and Arturo Fuente Opus X cigars to discuss his latest hypothesis on space aliens making regular visits to earth. I'd never asked what prompted his thinking or how he'd become obsessed with the subject. It didn't matter to me—I enjoyed controversy and spending time with my best friend, more actually stated, my only friend. The more we argued his theories, the further into fantasy his suppositions became. Lately, he'd been stuck on the postulation that extraterrestrials walked amongst us without anyone leaving a clue they had visited. Jack appeared rational when he presented premises supporting his presupposition, but I was beginning to question his state of mind.

Normally, we mixed backgammon with our back and forth, give and take discussions, but on this particular evening we stayed away from the backgammon table as Jack pointed to more comfortable chairs. I suspected Jack didn't want distractions during tonight's discussion. We'd been at it a couple of hours when I asked, "Jack, if we are visited by beings from another world, why don't we see or hear them?"

"These celestial travelers register on our sensors, i.e. eyes, ears, and so on, but they have the ability to block the collected data from being processed—our brain doesn't receive the information, so we don't know they exist."

I swirled the cognac to release its bouquet, and then lifted the snifter to my nose, savoring the fragrance of fine old grapes climbing the snifter walls before allowing a small amount of the $300 cognac to spill into my mouth. I let it lay on my palate for several seconds delighting in the flavor of the very special brandy for several seconds before letting it trickle past my gullet. After returning the snifter to a chair-side table I took a pull on my cigar and said, "Okay, for the sake of furthering the discussion, I'll concede your point; they have the ability to block what we see and hear from our minds, but if they steal from us, as you unabashedly proclaim, why don't we miss what they take?"

"For the same reason we don't see or hear them. They erase all traces of their activities from our brain. As far as we know, we were never in possession of the things they took. If all records of the things taken from us have been removed from our minds, then, as far as we are concerned, these items never existed.

"So, one might be in the room with us drinking your brandy and smoking your cigars?"

"Exactly."

Jack had never gone this far during our discussions of his suppositions; perhaps he had previously been concerned I would laugh at him.

Jack very rarely joked, so it was no surprise that he had his serious face on when he refreshed our snifters with a wee dram of Remy Martin, returned to his plush Paloma leather chair, leaned back, propped his feet on the ottoman, took a long breath through his seventy-five-dollar Arturo Fuente Opus X Robusto Colorado, and exhaled the smoke slowly. He was obviously hesitant to make his next statement or perhaps ask another question. A few more seconds passed before he took in another deep breath, let it out slowly, and then asked, "Dan, have you noticed the general population is becoming more and more corpulent?"

"Yeah, every day, and I don't have to leave home to be reminded, but what does that have to do with space aliens?"

My comment, although true—Sandy was a size four when we married and now wore eighteen-sized dresses—it was meant to be funny.

Jack continued as though I hadn't responded. "You're familiar with feedlots, right?"

"Sure, cattle are fattened in feedlots before they're shipped to slaughterhouses."

"Precisely. So, what if extraterrestrials use Earth as a feedlot?"

"Jack, I think your brandy must be of a higher proof than I realized."

He ignored my comment, took another deep breath, let it out and then began making his case. "I'm serious, hear me out and consider what I have to say before you start laughing, okay?"

"Hey, I'm susceptible to wild theories—go for it."

"Alright then: I have given this considerable thought, and I believe extraterrestrials fatten Earthlings and return on a regular schedule and harvest everyone who reached whatever weight specifications they have set for us."

"Okay, let's say I buy into your theory, where do these space aliens live? How do they get to Earth?"

"I don't know. But look at it this way. What do we really know about space travel? A century ago, did anyone seriously believe someone from Earth would walk on the moon?"

"I'm sure some did. I suspect when Galileo looked to the heavens, he dreamed of the day we humans would fly to the moon. I can't speak for kids in Galileo's day or a hundred years ago, but I was influenced by something I read way back when, 'Anything the mind can conceive and reasonably believe can be achieved.' So yes, I figured Flash Gordon would make it someday."

"Dan, you're making my case for me. If we humans can make '. . . one giant leap for mankind.' by walking on the moon, then on what basis can we suppose other civilizations from other worlds in other solar systems or perhaps even other galaxies aren't capable of space travel? Why should we believe these civilizations haven't developed space travel far beyond anything we can envisage? Is it inconceivable the seeds of humanity were planted here on Earth by an alien civilization a million or so years ago for the very purpose of having a ready-made and easily accessible food supply—a food supply that is now coming to fruition for them?"

"I understand where you're coming from, but how do they force people to overindulge and become obese without first having programmed them? Also, why have these aliens waited so long to begin harvesting?"

"Programming could be part of how they do it, but I think it's much simpler. However, programming our minds could be used in conjunction with my theory. As for the second part of your question: '. . . why have these aliens waited so long to begin harvesting?' How do we know they've just begun? Logic would tell us they were waiting for their food supply to swell, to multiply, until there were enough fattened up humans to make harvesting worthwhile. The preserving of food began ten to fifteen thousand years ago when man learned to dry food. Persevering food by canning began in the late eighteenth century. There were no fat people back then because all their time was spent gathering enough food for the next day or two. With the techniques for food preservation today, combined with the amount of leisure time we have due to modern labor-saving devices, the harvesting of humans has become worthwhile to these alien visitors."

"'How do we know . . . ?' I'll accept that part of your argument— if your theory holds true; we wouldn't know. You mentioned using a method of fattening-up people simpler than programming our minds, what might that be?"

"What if they have genetically modified our food to keep us craving high-caloric diets? Would that not produce the same result as having cattle continuously eating while standing around in a feedlot all day?"

"I suppose it would. So, what are you saying?"

"Let's take it to another level?"

"Okay, you're the man, take me there."

"What if space aliens own fast-food chains, as well as all-you-can-eat buffets and keep the prices low to encourage earthlings to overeat? Wouldn't that serve as a feedlot?"

"Oh, come on Jack. According to your theory, they prevent our brain from allowing us to realize they exist. So how could they own a restaurant without exposing their hand?"

"If they have the ability to block their existence from our minds, couldn't they allow us to see and interact with them if they so choose?"

"I guess so. But that would mean they look just like us and would make them cannibals."

"Not necessarily. If they can prevent us from seeing or hearing them whenever they want and on the other hand interact with us whenever they choose, couldn't they present themselves as human or for that matter, in any form they want us to see? As far as cannibalism goes: if they were of a different species—a fact we must accept since they are from another world—wouldn't eating humans be the same for them as eating Chateaubriand is for you and me?"

"You have a point. I'll give it some thought. I'm sure I'll have more questions for you when we continue discussing your feedlot theory the next time we get together."

"Does that mean you find my theory credible?"

I took a long draw on my cigar, flipped the ash into a heavy crystal ashtray, and slowly exhaled the smoke before I answered his question. "Jack, having lived for three-quarters of a century,

I've come to believe nearly anything is possible. I can't say I find it plausible, but your argument is persuasive. Have you encountered anything tangible that has led you to believe this feedlot speculation of yours to be true?"

"No, only images flashing on the backside of my eyelids. When it first happened, I was reminded of the old axiom, 'Your life flashes before your eyes when you are dying.' However, I wasn't dying and the images I saw had nothing to do with my life."

"What images?"

"Promise you won't laugh?"

"I won't laugh—I promise."

"Okay, I'm going to hold you to your promise."

He hesitated a moment or two and then continued.

"I first noticed the images when I closed my eyes, while on my way home sitting in my car waiting on a traffic light. I'd spent most of the afternoon at my desk working on a Microsoft Office Power Point document I would submit to the board outlining and amplifying changes I had proposed at the last meeting. My eyes were tired, so, I leaned back, intending to rest them for a few seconds—I figured someone would lean on their horn when the light turned green. Just before I closed my eyes a rotund couple stepped off the curb and began waddling across the intersection. When I closed my eyes, I was still looking at the scene that had been in front of me before I closed them, with the fat people about a quarter of the way across the intersection.

While contemplating this weirdness, the two obese people disappeared from the picture on the back of my eyelids. Startled I opened my eyes. Nothing had changed in the intersection other than the two portly people had vanished. I closed my eyes again. Everything went dark, just as you would expect."

"Jack, I think you need to layoff off the brandy."

"I knew you would laugh."

"I'm not laughing, but I do think you've been working too hard."

"Well, could be: for the last six months I've put a lot of time into revamping my company, trying to keep it in the black without having to let any of my employees go. These are stressful times, but the pictures I glimpse when closing my eyes started long before all these new federal regulations put my company in jeopardy. It's always the same, I'm watching fat people, usually on the street when I'm in transit between home and office, I close my eyes and find I'm still looking at the scene in front of me. A second later the obese people disappear. I open my eyes, and everything is the same other than the overweight people are no longer there.

"Sometimes I think I'm going crazy, but I'm not. I've never done dope—I'm not hallucinating. I never drink alone, so I'm not drunk when I'm going to work or coming home—you're my only friend and the only person I drink with. Dan, have you ever seen me drunk?"

"No! We have dinner at the club most evenings, and we share a bottle of wine with meals. Even though the club stocks wines especially for us, we never have a second bottle. So, I can honestly say I've never seen you the least bit tipsy."

"I know you are telling the truth and not saying something you know I want to hear just because of our friendship. So, this leaves only two options: either my theory is correct or I'm losing my sanity."

Jack leaned back deep into his chair, took a long slow draw on his cigar, and let it out slowly before asking, "Dan, do you think I'm crazy?"

Considering the fact that more than 70% of people age twenty or older are overweight with nearly 40% obese, Jack's theory made sense. Be-that-as-it-may, his feedlot theory weighed heavily on his mind at the moment and I feared it might drive him crazy. I would be going home soon and didn't want to leave him worrying about something he couldn't prove or change, whether true or not. So I took us back to our childhood.

"Not any crazier than when you talked me into sneaking up to Betty Sue's bedroom window to watch her undress and go to bed."

Jack smiled; we both smiled. "Yeah, those were exciting times, but she wasn't much to look at back then, huh?"

"No, not at ten years old, but a few years later I equated looking at her with a glimpse into heaven."

"For sure, but by then we were no longer standing outside looking in. She'd open the window so we could crawl inside. I sometimes wish I'd married her; don't know why I didn't."

"I've often had the same thoughts; I still think of her every day and often dream about her. I remember the best day of my life as though it were yesterday. The day the three of us were old enough to move into an apartment. We became the original Three's Company long before a TV program with that same name became popular."

"Dan, have you ever wondered what happened to her?"

"Oh yeah, even considered trying to find her, but figured she had a life and didn't need me messing it up for her."

"Yeah, me too, perhaps we should try to locate her. Who knows, she might be having the same thoughts about us as we have about her."

I had him thinking about the carefree days of our youth, so hopefully he'd go to bed and dream about our fun times with Betty Sue and not have nightmares about space aliens and disappearing fat people.

I breathed in the vapors trying to escape the snifter as I let the last of the cognac slide onto my palette—it lay there like velvet for a few seconds until I sent it on its way to join the rest of the fine elixir I'd consumed throughout the evening. I stuck the half-smoked Robosto Colorado in my mouth and stood.

"Jack, as always, I've enjoyed spending the evening with you—drinking your brandy, smoking your cigars, discussing your wild theories, and reliving our past, but I have an early appointment tomorrow and need to be rested when I meet with my client."

"I enjoy our get-togethers as well. I too have an early morning; I need to prepare for tomorrow's board meeting. I'll walk you to the door."

As we passed the media room, I noticed his television was on.

"Jack, I don't remember your TV being on when I arrived, are you hiding Betty Sue in there?"

"I wish." He laughed and then explained, "before you arrived, I was watching the know-it-all, pundits trying to guess what the market will do if the feds raise overnight interest rates. Guess I forgot to turn it off."

"Yeah, I have the same problem with forgetfulness. But considering we're getting older with every passing day and have no one around to remind us of things we need to do, I don't find it unusual a couple of old bachelors like you and me would forget things every-now-and-then."

Epilogue

What are memories: our personal history as we lived it . . . perhaps? Then again, maybe not, what if—yes, the world is full of "what ifs—our memory has been distorted, and parts of our past were removed and replaced? What if memory can be altered by a force unknown and beyond comprehension?

Did this unknown force expunge memories from the minds of Dan, and Jack? Is Betty Sue real or a fantasy to replace Louise and Sandy? Will she replace them? Did the wives ever exist?

Our dreams often take us to places we've never seen, and involves us in situations we've never known; are these minds-eye visuals conjured up subliminally, or is it possible they are residuals from parts of our lives removed by this super-natural force.

How would we know?

Eclipse – the story of a Horse, a Gambler, and a Madam

Victoria Hardesty
Author of Action, Adventure and Suspense with Arabian Horses

People who follow thoroughbred racing are familiar with the Eclipse Awards, which are voted on at the end of each year by the National Thoroughbred Racing Association (NTRA), Daily Racing Form, and the National Turf Writers Association. It is considered the "Oscars" of horse racing. It honors Champion Horses in 11 Divisions, Owners, Breeders, Trainers, and Jockeys and selects one outstanding horse for their Horse of The Year Award. Few know much about the horse this prestigious award is named for.

Eclipse was thus named because he was born April 1, 1764, the day of a solar eclipse from Spain to Scandinavia, at Cranbourne Lodge Stud owned by Prince William Augustus, Duke of Cumberland. Eclipse was a bright chestnut with a narrow blaze down his face terminating between his nostrils, and a high white stocking on his right rear leg. As he grew up, his rowdy attitude nearly got him castrated. At age 5, he stood just over 16 hands with his rump an inch higher than his withers. He was a large horse for his day with what many considered an "ugly head."

What piqued my interest the most is that Eclipse was the great-grandson of the famous Darley Arabian on his father's side and he was a grandson of the famous Godolphin Arabian on his mother's. I've owned Arabian horses for 34 years and am very partial to the breed. Eclipse was a part-bred Arabian.

The Duke of Cumberland died in 1765. The leggy yearling, Eclipse, passed through several owners including a meat farmer/ sheep dealer before half interest in him was sold to Dennis O'Kelly, an Irish gambler, scrapper, womanizer and conman. One of his previous owners had enough of his testy attitude and hired a rough rider to put him through his paces. A brutal schedule of hard trotting during the day with "poaching runs" at night settled him down, or plain tired him out. No one was ever able to contain him, even under saddle during a race. His jockeys just sat down and held on. Eclipse loved to run!

Dennis O'Kelly came to England from a tiny town in western Ireland to seek his fortune. He found himself carrying Sedan Chairs for the rich and famous. He cultured a relationship with a wealthy benefactress that put coins in his pocket and the lifestyle he craved. Gambling was pervasive in all levels of society at that time. Wealthy women who found themselves cash poor often turned their fancy homes into gambling palaces to maintain their standard of living. O'Kelly discovered the joys of gambling. His benefactress introduced him to all the right people before she died. Not long later, during a stint in debtor's prison over gambling debts, he ran into one of the most famous "ladies of the evening" in the country, the brothel madam Charlotte Hayes. They began a partnership and romantic relationship that lasted until he passed away years later from overindulgence, more commonly called gout.

Eclipse began his racing career at the age of 5. Racing then was nothing like today. His first race was three heats of four miles. He won it without a serious challenge. Mr. O'Kelly laid out his down payment on a half interest in Eclipse after the first two heats that day. He supposedly also coined the famous phrase, "Eclipse first and the rest nowhere." Nowhere meant at least 240 yards behind.

Eclipse raced 18 times between 1769 and 1770, winning every race. Eight of those races were walkovers, meaning he had no competition. O'Kelly bought out the other half interest in Eclipse so he could keep all his winnings.

May 3, 1769, he ran four-mile heats to win at Epsom Downs, and on the 29th he ran two- mile heats to win at Ascot, earning fifty guineas (a guinea was one pound, one shilling) at each race, which was a King's fortune in those days. He ran four races in June that year, two in July and ended with one in September. He won the King's Plate in five of those races, 50 guineas in three of them and the City Silver Bowl in Salisbury his first year. In 1770, he ran two races in April, one in June and July, two in August, one in September and finished with two races in October, back to back on the 3rd and the 4th, earning another King's Plate. In ten of the King's Plate races, Eclipse carried 168 pounds, the highest weight that was carried by a winner in England up to 1840. He ran one Match Race in 1770 at Newmarket against the notable Bucephalus and won easily. O'Kelly was forced to retire him after October 1770 because no other horse would run against him and no one bet on the other horses anyway. Eclipse was widely known as the horse no one could ever beat.

During Eclipse's 17-month racing career, Dennis and Charlotte enjoyed the finer things in life. They set up housekeeping in

Middlesex in a lovely country home where they entertained lavishly. It is interesting to note their former home became the prim and proper North London Collegiate School for Girls.

When Eclipse retired in 1770, things only got better for them. Eclipse stood at stud early on for 10 guineas per mare, which increased, rapidly to 50 guineas per mare. He earned the couple close to Thirty Thousand Pounds, or Six Million Dollars in today's money. Some of that came from racing, but a good amount came from breeding. Eclipse bred over 300 mares at 50 guineas apiece, which is the equivalent of $10,000 per mare now.

Eclipse kept breeding despite the fact his feet gave out on him and he foundered. Probably the first "horse-box," or horse-trailer, was created to move him from mare to mare around England in relative comfort. Ultimately, Eclipse suffered an attack of colic at age 24 and passed away a couple of years after O'Kelly. Eclipse left a legacy of fine horses behind. It is estimated that 95% of today's Thoroughbred horses trace directly back to him through their male tail line.

A necropsy, or animal autopsy, was done on Eclipse when he died. The doctors found his heart weighed an exceptional 14 pounds. This same "X-Factor" applied to two of his most famous descendants, Secretariat and Phar Lap.

After Eclipse died, pieces and parts of him spread far and wide. His tail hairs became ornaments, and his hooves became inkwells, five of which have surfaced to date. His bones shuffled around a bit before they finally landed at the Royal Veterinary College near Hatford in England. They've studied his bones and DNA from his teeth to find out what made him such an exceptional horse. Dr. Alan Wilson, who was in charge, said: "All the factors for speed perfectly matched. A key ability for a fast horse is to be able to bring its legs forward quickly, which is difficult for large animals with long limbs. Eclipse was smaller than modern racehorses. Rather than being some freak of nature with incredible properties, he was actually just right in absolutely every way."

Flyboy
The Story of a Kansas Farm Boy Turned Pilot
Victoria Hardesty

Author of Action, Adventure and Suspense with Arabian Horses

I married John Dewey Hardesty, Jr. in 1972. I didn't know much about his family when we married because he was an only child and both his parents had been dead for several years when we met. Over the years I learned bits and pieces about Jack's family (I'm going to stick my neck out here. Who takes a perfectly good four-letter name and "shortens" it to another four-letter name? President Jack

Kennedy, Jack Hardesty, etc. And, when Jack was young, they shortened his given name to five letters to call him Jacky!)

Jack's father, John Dewey Hardesty, was a Kansas farm boy. When WWI broke out in 1915, he and thousands of other young men went to their local Army Recruiter and signed up. Dewey, as the family called him, was shipped to Brownsville, Texas and assigned to the U.S. Army Corps of Engineers. When his basic training was complete, he shipped off to his duty assignment in Toures, France.

The Army Corps of Engineers was responsible for docks, bridges, and airfields. They built them, repaired them, and maintained them. As a Kansas farm boy, he had little experience with any of them. We speculate he was involved with the airfield construction. He became familiar with early combat flying in France, and it changed the entire course of his life.

Dewey returned to Kansas from France in 1918. He worked and saved his money for three years before taking off for St. Louis, Missouri. In 1921, St. Louis was a hotbed of young aviation enthusiasts. We have Dewey's logbooks showing he began taking flying lessons in 1921. He bought his own plane and took any job he could find that put gas in the tank so he could fly. He did mail runs, parcel runs, and when things looked grim, he flew into cornfields in the Midwest and took passengers up for short flights for a few dollars and dinner.

We have family photos of him and two other flyers leaning on the Spirit of St. Louis with Charles Lindberg. We have a couple of old photos of him and his friends working on his plane on the St. Louis airfield. He got involved in air races where 10 to 20 pilots left California airfields for flights to St. Louis and back. This was all done through visual flight rules because radar was not available on small planes at the time. His mother kept newspaper clippings that showed Dewey's progress each day during those races. We have most of those clippings from the Wichita newspaper. He won a couple of the races.

Dewey flew into a cornfield in Northern Kansas one day and took a young lady up for a flight over her small town. He liked her and pursued her, finally convincing Ora Pearl Fridley to marry him. With a wife to support, he persuaded Ora to move to Southern California where he knew he could get a job with Northrup and build planes for other men to fly. Not long after arriving in California, Ora found herself pregnant with their only son. Sadly, Dewey had to sell his airplane to pay the hospital bill. He removed the ID plate from that plane, and we still have it.

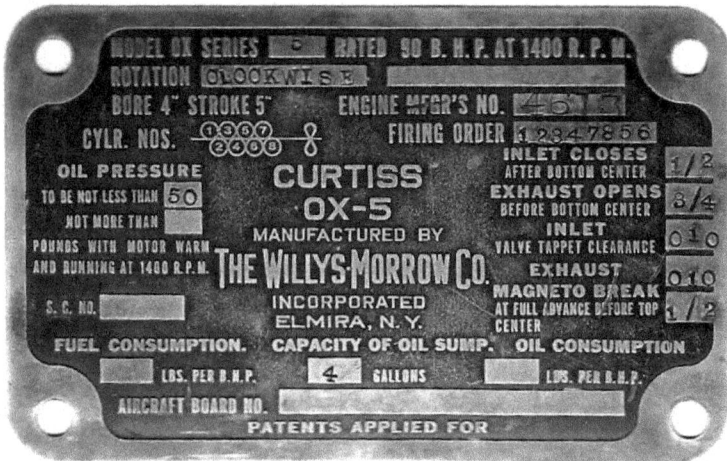

Ora was an experienced elementary school teacher. She applied to the Los Angeles Unified School District. They hired her for a career that lasted 37 years. She taught at an elementary school in Toluca Lake, California. At that time, the Toluca Lake area of Los Angeles was the home of many Hollywood movie stars, directors, and studio executives. It was close enough to get to Hollywood but provided the lavish lifestyle those people sought. Ora brought her son to school, so the children of the Hollywood elite were his classmates. One of his best friends was Gary Crosby, Bing's oldest son. Young Jack spent lots of time in the Crosby swimming pool with friends and future stars.

Dewey maintained friendships with early aviation pioneers throughout his life. We have one photo of young Jack climbing around the cockpit of "Wrong Way" Corrigan's plane. It was the very plane he landed in Dublin, Ireland by mistake (wink-wink), earning his nickname.

When World War II broke out, Dewey was too old to join the Army, but the Army Air Corps needed pilots. He volunteered. He had basic training at Long Beach, California, learning to fly the newer planes the AAC had at that time, from bombers to fighters. He based on the East Coast so he could fly the big bombers (B-17's) to England and return by ship for another plane. He flew fighter planes into North Africa during the campaign against Rommel. When the European Theater of War was over, he shipped out to Hawaii so he could fly fighter planes to Guam to fight the Japanese. He ferried back to Hawaii by submarine. We have one photograph taken on Christmas Day in 1944 on a submarine with him and several other pilots around a tiny Christmas tree. We also have coins he collected along the way from Europe, Africa, and the South Pacific.

When the wars were over, Dewey came home unsettled. He took a job for United Airlines in Denver and moved his family there briefly. His job was to train commercial pilots for United. That didn't give him enough time off the ground to suit him, so he left that job and moved the family to the Bay Area in California. He took a job with Pan American to fly their San Francisco to Tokyo runs. That kept him in the air more to his liking. The family moved back to Southern California so his wife could resume her teaching career. Dewey could hop a flight from Los Angeles to San Francisco so he could pilot the next commercial jet to Tokyo. All was good.

We have logs of those flights as well. He kept everything well documented. The flights to Tokyo had several stops along the way for fuel. But the trips were long and, for some pilots, grueling. For Dewey, they were just what the doctor ordered.

For most of their marriage, Ora and Dewey were together between flights. He missed a lot of time with his wife and only son. He was heading for Tokyo when his son graduated from high school. He stayed home for a couple of weeks when his Ora had cancer surgery; then he was off again. She never worried about him because his mistress was not another woman—it was flying. As long as he could fly, he was happy.

Dewey turned 65 years of age in 1966. That day was the end of his flying. The government canceled his pilot's license based strictly on his age. His job with Pan Am was over. He got his retirement and his gold watch, but it shattered his heart. He could never get his feet off the ground again. He began drinking heavily to dampen the pain. It took two years for his heart to stop beating. His spirit was free to soar. His wife joined him in 1970. My husband joined his parents in 1998.

As I look through the logbooks and see the places Dewey stopped over the years, my heart aches. He would have been a wonderful soul to get to know, but I know he is up there doing what he loved. I hope his wife and son are now doing it with him.

Grow Greener Spiritually

Rebecca Wetzler

Purposeful overcomer sharing the fruit of faith

Spring is just around the corner, a time when my grandmother used to search the barren, snow covered trees for the first pussy willows; a sure sign winter was on its way out. Once found, she would collect a few in a vase as if they were flowers.

Though she's been gone over 25 years, I still think of her and smile as those soft, gray buds appear. A little while after the pussy willows bloom, I start watching for one of my favorite signs: the day I can almost see a tinge of green on the trees; soon I can actually see the tinge of green on the trees; and then, almost overnight, the trees burst forth with lush green leaves.

It seems like nature imperceptibly peeks out, and then leaps into full bloom shouting spring's arrival. I love to see that transformation from gray to green, an annual affirmation of Genesis 1:11, 'Then God said, "Let the land produce vegetation: seed-bearing plants and trees on the land that bear fruit with seed in it, according to their various kinds." And it was so.'

It's amazing how small gardens, farm crops, entire forests begin as small seeds buried in soil. I admire people who have the green thumbs to tend beautiful yards, grow colorful vegetable or flower gardens, or work on farms producing our food. As for me, I cannot grow plants for long before they wither and die.

There are many things about growing plants I do not understand; one in particular is a little hard to wrap my mind around – organic fertilizers. It would never occur to me that plant and animal waste combined into a smelly stew would then be stirred into soil used to grow crops. I cannot help but grimace realizing I most certainly have unknowingly eaten vegetables plucked from such an unsavory mixture.

I have always thought waste is just that, waste, the unusable residue. While the title of one of Erma Bobeck's books is *The Grass is always Greener over the Septic Tank*, I thought it was simply a tongue in cheek metaphor rather than an actual phenomenon. However, turns out it is a real phenomenon, demonstrating residual plant and animal waste actually does have recyclable nutrients.

A caveat, though, is that greener grass can mean something good or something bad. It may just mean the leech field is providing the grass above it a little more water, nitrogen and phosphorous than the rest of the lawn; or it may mean the septic tank is leaking rather than leeching, and it will gradually create a bio-hazard swamp which will be unpleasant and expensive to deal with.

The bottom line for me, I will still eat my vegetables, but if I try planting flowers again, I will be buying my fertilizer at the local home improvement store and not make it myself with a backyard compost pile.

Figuratively, the backyards of our lives have personal compost piles which may be filled with broken dreams instead of crushed egg shells, heart wounds tossed in like orange peels, leftover relationship hurts added rather than dinner scraps, or stewing unforgiveness and anger akin to co-mingled waste residue.

How we care for our private unsavory mixture determines whether it leeches growth and wisdom or leaks hazardous consequences into our lives. To successfully use my personal compost, I need the Lord's guidance. In Matthew 13's 'Parable of the Sower' a farmer spreads his seeds on various ground surfaces, but only one is prepared to sustain growth.

First falling on a pathway, the seeds are quickly taken by birds; if one lacks understanding, the seeds of God's message are quickly swept away by worldly disbelief. Secondly, flipping seeds onto rocky ground may resemble where one initially starts understanding, but when believing causes trouble, the growth quickly withers, as it has no sustaining roots in faith. The next handful of seeds falls onto unkempt ground, where thorns of worldly worries and desires are able to choke out hope and trust in God's Word. Finally, seeds are planted in good soil; soil prepared to hear, understand, believe and follow God's Truth; soil that remixes lessons learned from unpleasant, difficult, and tragic events back into existing soil, continually strengthening the unwavering belief in God the Father, Son, and Holy Spirit; who is the Alpha and Omega, the Beginning and the End, and the Way, the Truth, the Resurrection, and the Life.

I am thankful I have chosen to tend to my personal compost pile versus abandoning it as I would for my poor plants. A lifetime of experiences mixed in with deliberate growth in knowledge of God's Word and faith in Jesus Christ has shown me that, though I may at first feel only imperceptibly hopeful in difficult circumstances, as I pray and seek His face my hope blooms full and colors my gray view with His Truth.

Then I can say with the Psalmist 'The LORD is my shepherd; I shall not want. He maketh me to lie down in green pastures: he leadeth me beside the still waters. He restoreth my soul: he leadeth me in the paths of righteousness for his name's sake.'

May I suggest you cultivate growing greener spiritually?

Honor

Carl Douglass: Neurosurgeon Turned
Author Writes With Gripping Realism

The scriptures ask, "What manner of men ought ye to be?"

My answer is, "I ought to be a man of honor. I ought to be a man who can honestly say, 'On my honor I will do my best to do my duty to God and my country, to obey the law, to help other people at all times. Like the famous 13 tenets of the Scout Law, I ought also to keep myself physically strong, mentally awake, and morally straight.'"

Examples:

1. On a narrow point on a dirt track road in Greece was found a stone with the following inscription: "Tell them in Lakedaimon, passerby: carrying out their orders, here we lie."

In 490 B.C. the Athenians at the battle of Marathon defeated the Persians, and the Persians were furious at having their great army defeated by a relatively small army of Greek warriors. Xerxes–Great King of Persia–rebuilt his army into the greatest fighting force ever mounted in history to that point of time. In 480 B.C., Xerxes brought his massive navy and army to the shores of the Greek Peloponnesus peninsula in preparation for a land march through Greece to the great city of Athens, which was unprepared to withstand the mighty Persians.

Xerxes' general Mardonius, demanded to meet Leonidas–military king of Sparta–to obtain a rapid surrender.

Mardonius said, "Our great army will take Greece. Surrender and become our slaves, and you will live."

Leonidas said, "Moven yabe," translated from the Greek to mean, "Come through me and take it."

Mardonius then said, "My archers will rain arrows on you such that they will block out the noonday sun."

To which Leonidas replied, "Then we will fight in the shade."

Mardonius returned to his army and prepared to march. Leonidas rallied the men of Sparta and several surrounding cities and rapidly moved into position in Thermopylae Pass with a total of only 1100 men. He chose a very narrow section of the four-and-a-half mile long pass to make his stand, barely wide enough for two men to walk side by side. On one side was the massive sheer face of the stone mountain, the Kallidhronon massif, and on the other was a 2,000-foot drop off into the gulf of Maliakos Kolpos and certain death below.

General Mardonius and his 200,000-man strong army advanced in a long line towards the Spartans. The men of the other cities aligned with Sparta either lost heart and fled or determined that they had to stay in their own cities to protect their wives and children. Finally, a mere 300 men–men of the royal guard–remained with Leonidas to frustrate the great Persian conquest of mainland Greece. The Greek defenders knew from the start that their efforts were tantamount to suicide; but they also knew that the course of Greek and–as it turns out–western civilization would be decided in the great struggle with the Persians; and it was crucial that they delay Mardonius long enough for Athens to prepare to defend Greece.

The Persians smashed into the Greek defenders and died by the thousands, having met the greatest warriors in the world, men for whom honor was everything. Again and again, the Persians pitted themselves against the short swords and shields of the Greeks only to be repulsed with huge losses. The numbers of Spartans were diminishing severely as well, and they were without food or water. Leonidas died on the second day, and the Spartans could only hold out for one more day. Finally, the great Persian army faced only one Greek soldier who could still stand up. He faced them with nothing but his sword. Persian archers readied their arrows. The angry Persian soldiers held their lances ready to finish off the lone remaining defender and waited for General Mardonius's final orders.

Mardonius looked at the last Greek left to defend Sparta's and Greece's honor and was about to give the signal to finish off the Spartan. However, Xerxes interceded and ordered Mardonius and his men to lower their weapons and let the Greek go free.

The great king is quoted as saying, "I wish I had an army of such men. If I did, I could conquer the world."

The delay provided by the Spartans gave Athens enough time to make their preparations for the battle. When it came three weeks later, the Greek city-states prevailed and saved not only Greece, but also the concept of the importance of the individual person, the cornerstone idea of Western Civilization. There are other versions of the Battle of Thermopylae Pass, but none of them diminish the heroism of the Spartan men of honor a whit.

2. Each year on April 30th, the French Foreign Legion has a parade across the Place de la Concorde, the largest square in Paris.

They carry a covered chest in which reposes a few medals, the cap of a Legionnaire officer, and a wooden hand. Few Frenchmen and almost no nonFrench know the significance of those items which are held in such great reverence by the Legion.

The story behind the curious collection of items is this: Between 1864 and 1867, a French dictator, Emperor Maximillian, ruled Mexico. In 1863, a Mexican rebel army was about to drive out the French and to regain sovereignty in Mexico. The 3rd company of Legionnaires led and protected a resupply convoy for the French army, fighting a withering series of battles along the way. Finally, by April 30th, the company had been reduced to 3 officers led by Capitaine Jean Danjou, and 62 NCOs and Legionnaires. Woefully undermanned, they watched as the mighty Mexican army advanced towards them. Danjou led his men into the ruins of a village called Camerone.

At 5 AM the Mexican army of 800 regular cavalry and 3 regular infantry regiments—2000 men—surrounded the mud brick buildings of the village. The Mexican general sent an emissary demanding the surrender of the French. Capt. Danjou lined his men before him. They were out of food and water and had only very limited ammunition.

He asked his men, "If you wish to save yourself, step back."

Not a single legionnaire moved.

Danjou made his reply to the Mexican general's demand for surrender, "Out of the question."

A Mexican bugler sounded the call "No quarter asked and none given." The cavalry attacked at 7 o'clock. Danjou was killed in the original onslaught. At 11, Sous Lt. Velam was killed. By 5 o'clock in the afternoon, only Sous Lt. Maudet and 12 Legionnaires were left alive. Mexican colonel Milan cursed his soldiers for allowing those few Frenchmen to hold off their army and ordered a full-frontal attack by his entire army. They stormed the yard, and within minutes, only Lt. Maudet and 4 Legionnaires remained alive. Among them they had only 4 cartridges left. Colonel Milan demanded that the Legionnaires surrender.

Lt. Maudet, echoed Danjou's reply, "Out of the question."

The handful of Legionnaires stood with fixed bayonets facing an army. Colonel Milan gave the order. Lt. Maudet was shot twice. Legionnaire Catteau stepped to the front to take charge and was stabbed 19 times in the next Mexican attack. That left 3 Legionnaires, all wounded, to face a force of 3000 rifles.

Mexican Colonel Combas then interceded, ordered his men to point their bayonets towards the sky, and halted the slaughter.

He walked to the 3 Legionnaires and said to them, "I can refuse nothing to men like you."

He then escorted the 3 wounded Legionnaires to his superior officer, Col. Milan, who said, "This is all that are left? These are not men but demons."

The fight for the honor of France by Capitaine Danjou's small battered force saved the convoy and gave France three more years to rule Mexico.

In 1892, the Mexican government allowed Napolean III of France to erect a small monument in the ruins of Camerone. The Latin inscription on the monument read: "Those who lie here, though less than 60 in number, fought an entire army before being overwhelmed by sheer weight. Life abandoned these French soldiers before honor did on 30 of April, 1863."

3. In 1991, a memorial headstone was placed in the location of a former Japanese internment camp in Weifang, China. It contained only a partial inscription taken from Isaiah 40:31, "They shall mount up with wings as eagles; they shall run and not be weary." No name was placed on the headstone.

This is the rest of the story: Eric Liddell was born in 1902 in Tienjin, China of Scottish missionary parents and was sent to England to school when he was eight years old. In 1924, while attending the University of Edinburgh, he proved himself to be a remarkable sprinter; and, he and his friend, Harold Abrahams, a

Jew, were chosen along with three others to represent Great Britain in the 1924 Olympics in Paris.

On the boat taking the team and British dignitaries to Paris, he learned that his heat in the 100-meter dash was scheduled to be run on a Sunday. Eric was a very devout Christian, and the scheduling caused a serious dilemma for him. If he ran in the heat, he would almost surely be the gold medalist in the Olympics. He would also fail in his Christian duty if he did so. The schedule could not be changed. The team coach and the British royal sponsor of the team, the Prince of Wales, placed enormous pressure on Eric to run the race, to make an exception to his perceived Christian duty, "this one time". However, for Eric, that was a failure and a sin beyond what he would permit himself. He steadfastly refused to run in the heat and gave up his chance for a medal.

However, his friend and teammate, Lord Andrew Lindsay, had already won a silver medal in his Olympic race, and he graciously offered Eric his place in the 400-meter race, which was scheduled to be held on a Tuesday. Eric gratefully accepted the offer. On the Sunday in question he delivered a sermon in the Paris Church of Scotland. He closed the speech by quoting the entirety of Isaiah 40:31, "But they that wait upon the Lord shall renew their strength; they shall mount up with wings as eagles; they shall run and not be weary; and they shall walk, and not faint."

Eric Liddell ran in the 400-meter race and in the finals. He beat the highly favored American competitors to win the gold medal, and in so doing, set a world record that lasted for four years. Thereafter, Eric was called the "Flying Scotsman".

He returned to China as a missionary in 1925 and served as a teacher. China's history between then and 1941 was violent and frightening. In 1941, Japanese conquerors approached the city where Eric was laboring. The British government ordered all British Nationals to leave the country, and his wife and children were evacuated to Canada. He never saw them again. Liddell, however, refused to leave and accepted a position in a rural station in

Northern China to serve the poor. In 1943, the Japanese overran the town and herded all of the inhabitants into an internment camp in Weihsien, later called Weifang.

Eric became the de facto camp temporal and spiritual leader. Many of the missionaries and priests hoarded food for themselves from the black market and entered into corrupt deals with the Japanese to save themselves at the expense of the poor Chinese. Eric refused to eat while others starved or to discriminate against the poor Chinese peasants and scolded his fellow Christians. He shared his meager rations and worked tirelessly to help all the internees in the camp. Along with them, he starved and became sick. On February 21, 1945 he died of an untreated malignant brain tumor. Just before he was about to die, the Japanese offered him the unique privilege of being rescued from the camp by the British. He did not leave. Only many years later was it learned that Eric Liddell had given his place of rescue to a pregnant Chinese woman.

A headstone was placed on his grave during the 60th year celebration of the day that the Japanese were driven out of the Weifang Internment Camp. His children directed that the stone not contain his name, since he was such a modest and self-effacing man during his life. The Chinese government directed that it contain the quotation from Isaiah.

Hunting Is …

Evan Swensen

"Once you pull the trigger, the fun is all over."

"If you need to shoot something to make a hunting trip success-ful, you went for the wrong reasons."

"I didn't ruin the hunt by killing something."

These statements reflect an attitude expressed by hunters who come back skunked. In part they attempt to justify or rationalize for the lack of game. Perhaps we have all used one or more of these excuses. I know I have.

Looking back with a 60-year Alaska hunting perspective con-firms a true-ism was spoken each time such a statement was made.

Hunting is more than shooting. Talk to any hunter or search your own memory, and I'll bet it's the other things and not the shooting that makes the hunt.

It's the fireside at day's end, the northern lights shooting searchlight beams of color across a star filled night sky, the full moon changing mountaintops from dark shadows to ice white temple spires.

It's campfire smoke in your eyes, blisters on your feet, bugs in your soup, and rocks under your sleeping bag. It's a rainbow after a storm, waking to the deafening silence of new snow, or just lying in your sleeping bag watching your breath on a cold morning.

It's not shooting that makes the hunt. It's not shooting that makes a person a hunter. He may have a scrapbook filled with photos or walls lined with trophies.

He may own airplanes, boats, campers, and snow machines to get him afield. He may have hunted Africa, Asia, and Alaska. Rifles, shotguns, and pistols may fill his gun cabinet.

He may have received awards, citations, and honors. Still it's the other things he remembers and speaks about.

Our family has its share of game in the freezer each winter.

When the meat is prepared and dinner is served, we remember, rehearse, and enlarge the size of the pack, the distance of the hike, and the quality of the cooking—not the shooting.

Hunting begins with planning and packing, replanning and repacking.

If the hunter goes for the wrong reasons, the hunt only ends when the trigger is pulled.

The size or number of animals taken does not measure hunting success.

It is measured by the sum of all the parts from concept to completion.

Hunting Is More Than Shooting

Evan Swensen

Fishing or hunting trips seldom go exactly as scheduled nor do they always end up with a full freezer. As an example, my daughter, Diane, and I were hunting goats just before her 18th birthday. It rained a steady downpour the entire second day of the hunt. A cold wind blew rain against us with such force our rain gear finally surrendered and let the water in. We became so cold it hurt. Finally we could stand it no longer. At 5 in the afternoon we gave up and pitched our tent, deciding to just hole up and get dry and warm, thinking tomorrow has be a better day.

No sooner than the tent was up, the rain doubled its intensity and the wind picked up to gale force, driving the rain under the fly and right through the tent walls. We woke about midnight cold and wet. It made for a long night with very little sleep.

Several years ago I took two co-workers hunting. We flew out in my old Stinson on skis. After spending two days and a night we decided to move camp. Immediately after take off I ran out of altitude, airspeed, and ideas all at once. In the resulting crash we sustained injuries, but nothing life threatening or permanent. The airplane was wrecked and my pride was seriously hurt.

These two failed hunting trips really turned out to be successes. Like the night in the wet tent with Diane. At first light we climbed out of the sack, rung at least a gallon of icy water from each bag, and headed down the mountain to timber. Locating a perfect campsite, we made a lean-to, built a fire, got warm, and slept for the balance of the day. For the next two days we dried out gear. Although no more rain came in our camp the mountain where the goats were was constantly fogged in.

We didn't fire a shot the entire week, but it was one of our most memorable hunting trips. Enduring the cold and wet let us discover some things about each other and ourselves. We learned lessons about our abilities, our capabilities, and our frailties. I gained a greater respect for my teenage daughter. Her self-confidence increased. Some of the generation gap was closed.

My hunting companions in the crashed Stinson proved to be real sportsmen and friends. They did not file lawsuits or make threats. They were sensitive to my lost airplane and injured pride. They did not place blame or cast judgment. The airplane was not salvageable, but through their kindness, my feelings were repaired.

Time healed the wounded pride and the airplane was replaced. My hunting partners made me a gift of a new rifle to replace the one broken in the crash. I use this gun each hunting season. It serves as a constant reminder, not of the wreck, but of two hunters who were also great sportsmen.

It's Best To Park Your Car Above The High Tide Mark

Evan Swensen

Prior to the Great Alaska Earthquake the land along the shore of Turnagain Arm was as much as 8 feet higher. The earthquake slipped the earth's crust allowing the land at the mouth of 20-Mile Creek to sink. Before the earthquake I fished the area many times a season. A one-hour drive from Anchorage would put me on the creek. Ten minutes to slip the boat from its trailer and load up our gear, and another 15 minutes of river travel put us at an excellent silver fishing hole at the junction of 20-Mile and its first clear water tributary.

Our habit was to arise early, drive to the creek, dash to the tributary, fish for a couple of hours, and return home in time for work. An alternate schedule was to leave after work, do our fishing and return home before it got dark. We did this several times a week during the silver run. The limit was 6 fish and it didn't take long to supply our needs of fillets and smoked salmon.

One such day my fishing partner, Max Marquiss, and I arrived at the fishing hole in the early evening. As we pulled into the tributary and slid the boat up on the beach we discovered the water was boiling with migrating silver salmon. It was an evening when we almost had to bait our hook from behind a tree to keep the fish off until we could cast. In our exuberance we forget the time and fished until it was dark.

Wanting to remain over and catch the morning's first fishing we justified staying by making the excuse that we didn't want to go on the river at night. We pulled the 12-boat up on the beach, propped it up on its side for a lean-to, built a fire in front, and cooked a fresh-caught silver for dinner. Using spruce boughs for a bed we slept until it was light.

With the first light of morning we noticed that the water in the stream had come up during the night. We paid it little attention and went about fishing. Finally running out of time we left the stream so we could return home in time for work.

When we arrived back at our car we discovered that it had been flooded by the tide. We learned that the year's highest tide had occurred that night. Fortunately, water did not get into the gas tank, but the engine and seats had been covered. We drained the crankcase and flushed it out with kerosene, then filled it with oil. It started up and we let it run for a few minutes. We then reflushed it with kerosene and refilled the crankcase with oil, and sitting on wet seats we returned to Anchorage.

Immediately, the car was taken to a service station and given the full treatment. It was then run through the car wash several times. It seemed to run all right, and except for a foul interior smell it appeared that we had escaped with only a minor expense and a little inconvenience. With the coming of winter we soon learned we were mistaken. At the first day of freezing weather we found that water had gotten into many places and it remained even after service. Things that were supposed to slide didn't. Windows wouldn't roll up or down. The transmission wouldn't shift; the interior fogged up, and then froze restricting our vision.

Toward summer, when it seemed that all was well and we were now past any crisis, inconvenience turned to tragedy. First, the U-joints broke, then door windows handles refused to work, and finally the front wheels fell off. Upon careful examination we discovered that almost everything covered by the saltwater of Turnagain Arm was rusted away or corroded beyond use or repair. We had to junk the car.

I've only been back up 20-Mile once since the earthquake. The gravel beaches we fished from and camped on are now covered with mud. Because the land has lowered, the beach is now tide affected. No longer can Max and I siwash it on 20-Mile and fish all night for silvers, even if we remembered to keep our car above the tide line.

Liquorice All Sorts

Magdel Roets
Writer of Christian Fiction

Many years ago, my youngest daughter and I were shopping peacefully when a young man wearing what looked like a clown suit interrupted us.

"I see you have Liquorice All Sorts in your trolley," he said. I told him I do not often buy Liquorice All Sorts, trying to limit sweets as much as possible, though this was a favourite in my family, but that day was an exception because we were celebrating something. I cannot remember now what we were celebrating. Then the young guy gave us a ticket and said:

"Well, besides your celebration, it was a good day to buy Liquorice All Sorts. If you hurry over to the school's playfield across the street, you can present the ticket and have a free helicopter flip over the city, complements of Liquorice All Sorts". It was only then that I noticed his costume looked like an All Sorts kebab.

My daughter pushed our trolley into a corner and we hurried out of the shop just as the helicopter was landing to take up the next group of All Sorts fans. We duck to avoid the blades and climbed aboard. I was scared stiff as I fastened my seat belt but my daughter smiled as if she was flying every day. The chopper lifted off the ground, turned three-sixty degrees, yawed, banked and then went up high above the city. I started praying before we left contact with solid ground, clawing my seat as if I could keep us in the air by holding on to it.

Next thing I knew, it was like I could feel, tangibly, the hand of God holding the chopper and guiding it over the rooftops. At this I unwound, pressed my head against the window to get the best view of the city. Calm and relaxed I enjoyed the trip immensely. What an experience it was for someone who had not flown in any kind of aircraft in years, knowing that wherever I went, God is with me and He protects me always and everywhere.

After we stepped out of the helicopter, my daughter and I went back to the shop to resume our shopping, loaded two extra packets of All Sorts and ate one on our way back home. I hope my daughter has the same fond memories of that day as I have.

When my nerves try to get the better of me with this coming trip to Abu Dhabi, I just think back on that day in the heli and I calm down right away. God's hand is there, ready to take the airplane in His hand and bring us to Abu Dhabi and back safely. His Name be praised.

Mrs. Zucherberg

Cil Gregoire
Alaska Si-Fi Queen

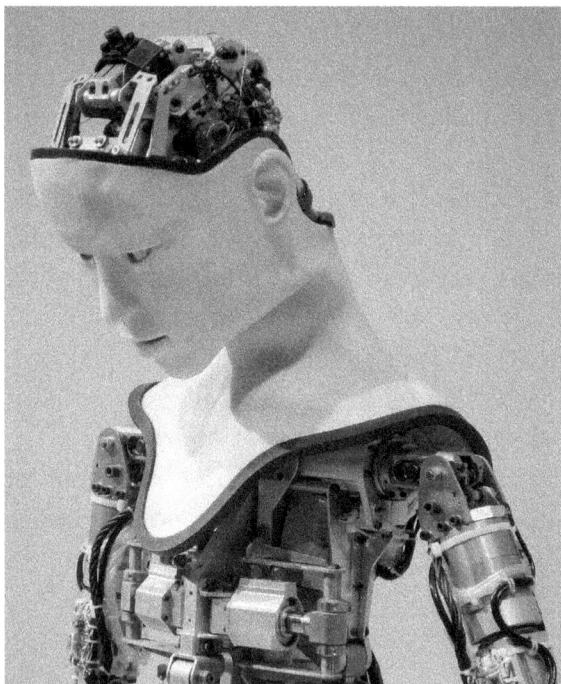

Agnes Zucherberg was born in 1997. Today is her birthday. She is 103. Nurse Alice entered her room triggering the simulation of the dawning of a new day. The images of stars faded from the walls and ceiling as the room brightened.

"Good morning, Mrs. Zucherberg. Rise and shine." She set the breakfast tray down on the table and helped Mrs. Zucherberg sit up. "Happy Birthday," she said setting the breakfast tray in front of her. "Look, the 3-D printer printed out breakfast sausage as a special birthday girl treat."

"Thank you," Agnes said. "Thank you for taking such good care of me."

"You are very welcome, Mrs. Zucherberg. Eat up. Your physical therapist will be here shortly." The room continued to brighten to full daylight. Soon after Nurse Alice picked up her tray, Physical Therapist Margaret entered the room.

"Happy Birthday, Mrs. Zucherberg. Where would you like to go today? Would you like to take a walk through the gardens or along the beach?"

"A walk on the beach sounds refreshing." Physical Therapist Margaret attached bands around Mrs. Zucherberg's ankles and wrists and led her into the corridor. The bands emitted a force field to support Agnes so she could easily walk upright. The floor of the corridor appeared as golden sand. The right wall projected gleaming blue water lapping gently onto the beach. The left wall projected sand dunes, beach grass, and palm trees.

"Oh look, there's a sailboat!" Agnes exclaimed pointing out into the distance. "My Albert and I used to love sailing."

"It is indeed a beautiful day for sailing," Physical Therapist Margaret agreed. After a long pleasant stroll in the warm sea breeze, breathing the invigorating fresh air, Agnes was returned to her room.

Soon Nurse Alice arrived with her lunch, which included a small birthday cake richly decorated. "Your daughter Mildred will be arriving shortly for a visit. You can save the cake to share with her."

After lunch, Mildred arrived as expected. "Happy Birthday, Mother! How are you doing today?"

"Probably better than expected," Agnes said. "What do you have there?" she asked referring to the gift-wrapped box Mildred carried.

"It's a birthday present. Here, open it."

Agnes ripped off the wrapping and opened the box to reveal a small iridescent blue cube. "What is it?"

"It's the latest 3-D game. Place the cube on the table and press the four corners." Agnes loved games. She quickly activated the cube. The cube flattened out and expanded covering the entire surface of the table, then projected upward to reveal a complex game board.

Agnes and Mildred spent the afternoon drinking tea, eating birthday cake, and conquering the challenges of the 3-D game. At long last Mildred kissed her mother goodbye.

Mildred walked down the corridor to her room. Upon entering, she approached her dressing table, deactivated her head, carefully detached it from her body, and placed it on a stand. She picked up Nurse Alice's head, attached it to her neck, and activated it. Then she opened the closet door labeled "Nurse Alice" and changed her clothes before heading to the food dispenser to take Mrs. Zucherberg her dinner.

Noisy as a Raven

Victoria Hardesty

Author of Action, Adventure and Suspense with Arabian Horses

I've lived on our ranch in the Mojave Desert of Southern California for nearly 30 years now and Spring is the time of the year I love to watch the birds.

The birds around the ranch that have been the most interesting and fun to watch have been the California Ravens.

No, these are not Crows. Ravens are about twice the weight on average and stand between 18- and 24-inches head to tail. Their beaks are thicker, and they soar and dive on the thermals. They also have a different language with many interesting sounds. In flight, their tails are not straight across, they fan out in an arc. And they have a sense of humor.

We have a dog on the ranch whose mother was a Rottweiler, sired by what we suspect was a Jack Russell Terrier. She loves chasing rabbits and we see her boing-boinging through the brush when she's trying to catch one.

She loves to chase the Ravens. They love to play games with her. One Raven will sit on the arena fence, well within her reach, and caw at her until she gives chase. That bird will fly across the arena 3 feet off the ground and pull up and sit on the top edge of the barn, staring at her and cawing and clucking until she gets there.

She jumps up barking like she's going to catch that bird until it flies off and lands on a corral fence 50 yards away, again within her reach from the ground. It sits cawing at her until she gets just close enough before it flies to another part of the ranch, perches and waits, calling for her, and I suspect, laughing at her. I've watched that bird-and-dog chase go on for quite a while until one of them gets tired and flies off or heads back to the porch for the shade.

We've had several pairs of Ravens nest on the property. We've watched them build their nest of sticks, dry brush, grasses and whatever looks like building material to them. They laid their eggs and one parent sat on the eggs continuously.

They are notorious nest robbers themselves, so they are very protective of their own. One parent would be off hunting or doing whatever Ravens do for a few hours and return to the nest so the other can leave and do the same.

You can't tell one from another because they really all do look alike. They are black, shiny, and big.

They are the garbage men of the desert, so we see them on the road cleaning up carrion from roadkill.

Once the chicks hatch, they maintain that one-parent-always-with-the babies-schedule until the babies are about ready to leave the nest. They feed the babies a lot. In a few weeks the babies are nearly the size of their parents.

First flight for the baby Ravens is a joy to watch. We had one pair who nested on top of the electrical equipment at the top of a telephone pole. That was 40 to 50 feet above the ground.

Alpha Baby was very interested in leaving home as he matured and was the first one on the edge of the nest looking around. He was the first one who attempted to flap up to the cross bar at the top of the pole.

The second one was more timid. It took him another day or two before he tried to join his sibling on the cross bar. Little Sister was the most timid about getting to the edge of the nest and took two or three days more to try for the cross bar.

Alpha Baby was the first one to try out his wings. He jumped off the cross bar and soared about 75 feet away from the pole and landed with a small thud in the center of our round pen.

He flapped his wings, ruffled his feathers and strutted like he was king-of-the-walk. He was proud of himself for flying, even though the landing was a bit crude.

He hopped up on the top rail of the six-foot high round pen and called his brother who did the same flight, landing with a thud in nearly the same spot. He couldn't get the hang of how to perch on the bottom rail of the round pen. He kept falling off.

He walked over to the Juniper tree outside the round pen and flapped his way to the top of that.

Little Sister spent the entire night up on the cross beam alone. She wasn't ready yet. Neither parent stayed with her. She crash-landed in the Juniper tree the next day.

I watched Alpha Baby strutting on the ground like he was the Little Prince while she shuddered on that Juniper for several hours before she was ready to take to her wings again.

The parent birds talked to their babies until they finally got all three in the air. They took them up for their soaring lessons in the thermals several hundred feet above the ranch.

We had another clutch of three Ravens born in a 40-foot pine in front of our house. The babies flew from tree to tree, crash landing but improving each time as they tested their wings.

I watched one parent bird take the three babies up for their first soaring lesson. The last one in that group, I called the Fighter Pilot, was at the back of the pack when he turned sideways to the ground for some reason. Then he turned upside down and was headed straight for the ground.

I held my breath. I was afraid he was going to hit the ground and that would be the end of him. Then I watched him catch himself, turn over and struggle from about 6 feet from the ground. He headed back into the air.

He flapped like a demon to catch up with his parent and siblings, but he did it. Watching those four birds find a thermal and begin to soar was beautiful to see.

We still have several of those babies here at the ranch. They tend to stick around where they were born, sometimes for years.

We have one who injured his right leg. When he flies over the house, you can hear him coming and passing over. If you look up, you can see that right leg dangling and swinging in the breeze while his left leg is tucked up under his tail as it should be.

He still manages to eat, fly, and do what Ravens do.

He's been here for two years now, so the leg must not be bothering his eating, hunting, and getting around. He perches on the one leg at the top of the telephone pole, using his wing to prop up the injured leg.

We hope he'll be around for a long time, find a mate, and have his own brood here.

I'm always envious when I watch them soar. How would it feel to leave the ground and fly with the wind?

Norbert Crosskill and the Dodge Challenger

Mary Ann Poll
America's Lady of Supernatural Thrillers

From Kat Tovslosky, the main character in the Iconoclast Thriller series:
I am the part-time (and only) help for the Ravens Cove police.
In the winter, I go in once or twice a week.
So the story that follows can only be described as serendipitous.

The day started normally enough. As always, I stood in front of the station and fumbled through my bag for the ever-elusive keys. (I know I should put them in a specific pocket but it is winter in the Cove and ever-so boring.)

So, I made up this little game: I see how fast I can dig the keys out of my 'bottomless pit' of a purse. I reward myself with a mocha if I retrieve the keys in less than thirty seconds.

I grabbed the key ring on the first try. Exhilaration coursed through my body, and I high-fived my reflection in the door.

The sound of tires screaming to find traction on the frosted streets caused me to drop my prize back into the ebony depths.

I swung around to watch a fire-engine red Dodge Challenger speed toward the station—and me.

Terror replaced exhilaration in 'two shakes of a cat's tail,' as Grandma Tovslosky was fond of saying when she was alive.

I plastered my body against the door and sucked in my stomach. (Like that would make me less of a target?) All the things I hadn't done, all the things I'd yet to do flashed through my mind like an accelerated movie. *I'm really gonna miss mochas,* I thought.

I turned my head to the side and closed my eyes. I waited for the end to come.

Tires sliding like skates on ice filled my ears. Then silence.

I opened my eyes to see the Challenger sitting pretty as you please in front of the general store, which is about ten feet from the police station—and me. Still plastered to the door, eyes as wide as saucers, I watched Norbert Crosskill open the driver's door and slam the tip of his white cane to the ground. Norbert has been legally blind for at least a decade.

"Mornin', Norbert?" I couldn't think of anything else to say—well I could but it shouldn't be printed here.

He jumped. "Kat? Where'd you come from?"

"It's a work day for me," I replied.

Norbert dropped his head to his chest. "You know I'm not supposed to drive," he whispered.

"Yep."

He lifted his head and we stared at each. My eyes still wide from adrenaline, his wide as if it would help him see me better.

Norbert broke the silence. "Well, have a good day." He tap-tapped his way to the store and disappeared inside.

I located my keys and bee-lined it to my desk phone to call Bart. (Bart is my cousin and the town's police officer.)

I punched in the first three numbers and stopped. I couldn't shake the feeling that Norbert reached his boiling point that day and this reckless drive to town was his way of shaking a mental fist at his failing eyesight. I dropped the handset into its cradle.

"No harm, no fowl." I mumbled. I turned on the computer at my desk and went to work. Or, I should say, I tried to work.

My nerves would have none of this. I gave up and headed for home.

I cuddled into my overstuffed couch with a hot cup of some kind of nerve-calming tea and asked myself, "If Norbert is legally blind and, as far as I know, hasn't owned a vehicle in a decade, how did he get a car?"

I tapped the sides of my cup with one nail while I looked out the window. I let my mind dip and fly upward like a raven at play in the wind.

The light dawned and I bolted upright. I KNEW that car. (After all, I live in a small town and a fire-engine red Dodge Challenger kind of stands out.)

I promptly walked myself back to town and to the car's owner – namely Arnie Thralling who has a penchant for all motorized vehicles.

Arnie stood up straight when he saw me heading in his direction. He held up a hand and grinned. "I heard about that, um, incident from Norbert."

"Really? And you think it's funny?" I asked through gritted teeth.

Irritation turned to fury. It took everything in me to hold my tongue and not tell Arnie a thing or two about his character.

The smile left Arnie's face. "'Course not. I'll explain."

"Please do."

"Norbert came to me and said his niece would be visiting from somewhere South—Alabama, I think. He didn't want her to brave the elements, 'coming to such a cold climate and all.' So, I said no problem and dropped the car at his house."

"Okay . . .?"

Arnie shrugged. "The rest is history."

"Except for the fact that Norbert doesn't have a brother or sister, Arnie. How'd he get a niece?"

Arnie's eyes twinkled with new respect for Crosskill. "I never thought about that! Gosh, Norbert's still one shrewd guy."

"He's what? . . ." I stared at Arnie, still considering those few choice words. I let out a sigh. "Check the facts next time, would you Arnie?"

"Sure thing."

On the way home, I stopped at the top of Ravine's Ravine and looked back on the town. In that moment, the gift of living in Ravens Cove flooded my mind and heart. All the anger of moments ago dissipated. I smiled remembering what I loved about this place.

Both Norbert Croskill's and Arnie Thralling's actions spoke volumes about the personal views of all of our residents. We have to be creative and as independent as we can to live happily in small-town Alaska. It's about survival and helping each other to persevere.

"Even if it means letting your blind buddy drive your car," I whispered, then chuckled. "Well, creativity and independence are still alive and well here—I love this town!"

I turned on my heal and headed back into town to revel in its uniqueness—and to get me that well-deserved mocha.

Our Great Pyrenees Story

Victoria Hardesty
Author of Action, Adventure and Suspense with Arabian Horses
Author Mastermind Charter Member

The plight of animals in animal control facilities is more than tragic and the reasons for them being there, in many cases, is inexcusable. My husband and I spent eight years working with a rescue pulling victims of abuse, cruelty, and neglect and taking them to the rescue kennel. The director worked tirelessly to find them new homes. The dogs we pulled are more challenging to find homes for than most.

Michael and I volunteered for the Southern California Great Pyrenees Rescue. The dogs coming out of Animal Control shelters have a short time there because of their size. Five Chihuahuas stay in the same size kennel as one Great Pyrenees, and the feed requirements are about the same five to one.

Great Pyrenees dogs are fluffy white or marked white dogs that weigh in more than a hundred pounds for males and more than 90 pounds for females. We've seen one that topped the scales at 190 pounds, named Zeus. He looked like a white bear except for the wagging tail. He had feet in the quadruple-X large size, and his head was as broad as a steer. But he loved people!

Great Pyrenees dogs think for themselves. They guard their owner's property, livestock, and children from any intruder including bears, wolves, mountain lions, and creepy humans. They were initially bred by the shepherds in the Pyrenees Mountains to guard their flocks.

They do not move herds. That's the job of herding dogs. They go on duty at dusk and off at dawn. They alert at any sound they find unusual. Translated, they bark at night. They sleep most of the day. They go over five-foot fences in the blink of an eye. They decide what is friend and what is foe and they are smarter about that than their humans.

They are not bothered by hot or cold weather because of their double coats. They shed like crazy twice each year when they "blow out" their coats to grow new ones. They need regular grooming. They take up the entire couch or six square feet of flooring. They do not do well off leash in public because they tend to wander, especially the males. But, this breed forms attachments to their owners that are so special, they will do anything to protect them, even if it costs them their lives. They are sweet, loving, affectionate, and huge.

We had one occasion to pick up a four-year-old male in Bakersfield, California, a two and a half hour drive from home. We were to take the dog to the rescue kennel, another thirty-minutes in the opposite direction. With a lunch stop along the way, we expected this to take most of the day.

When we got to Bakersfield, the animal control officer asked us to breed-identify four puppies they'd picked up the previous day. He said they found them in a field eating carrion and they were throwing up. The vet hadn't seen the puppies yet. The AC personnel didn't know if they were throwing up because of what they ate or if they were sick. We immediately identified them as Pyrenees.

The officer offered to give us the puppies if we would take them to our vet, no paperwork or fees. We paid the bailout fee on the adult male and wondered how we were going to get him and four puppies back to San Bernardino in our small SUV. Those puppies needed help! They had almost no hair on their bodies from starvation. One puppy had no toes on one of his front feet. AC estimated them about six-months-old, and they were skin and bone. They were affection starved and desperately scared. But, being Pyrenees puppies, they were each the size of our 60-pound lab yearling. That was a lot of dog-flesh to stuff into our small SUV for the three and a half hour drive to the vet. We worried how the older male would take confinement with four active puppies.

We put the older dog in our vehicle first and carried the puppies one at a time. The dog sniffed each one as they came in. He was the best babysitter we could have. The puppies roughhoused in the back for the first 30 miles then laid down to sleep. Two of them gave me a near heart attack while they played and stepped on the electric window opener as I drove 70 miles an hour down the freeway. Mike handled the puppies while I rolled the window back up and set the child lock. The dog stayed up with the puppies and napped when the last puppy slept.

Puppies are like children. They sleep in short bursts. When they wake up, they need to relieve themselves. We were on a freeway with no collars and leashes for the pups and no safe place to turn off the road. One by one the pups woke, went to the back of the vehicle and peed. Once all four pups did their business, the older dog went to the same place and did the same. We had Lake Pyrenees in the back of our SUV!

I congratulated my husband for his purchase of the expensive rimmed cargo mat he bought. It saved our vehicle! We tossed the dog blanket it contained when we got home.

Our trip was in August. The temperature in Bakersfield was 112 when we left and 102 in San Bernardino when we pulled into the vet's parking lot. The air conditioning in our vehicle kept us comfortable. The doggie smell was a bit much, so we kept the front windows cracked for fresh air during the drive. The vet's office was closed for lunch when we arrived and not scheduled to open for an hour. We couldn't sit in our car, engine running and air conditioning on full blast, for that long with the dog and puppies in the back. The puppies were wide awake and wanted to play! None of them threw up during the drive, but more ominously, they hadn't pooped yet either.

Fortunately, this vet had a small unlocked yard beside the office for people and pets. We rushed the puppies, two at a time, to the dog yard and set them down before rushing back for the other two and finally the older dog.

No sooner did we set them down in the dog yard but they each pooped!

One of the employees came out the rear door heading for her lunch and saw us. She made arrangements for us to take the dogs inside the office right away.

We made our delivery and headed for home. We followed up with the director of the rescue. The puppies were diagnosed with early-stage Parvo Virus. They all survived. The older male was quarantined because of his contact with them but never got the disease. The puppy with no toes on his front foot suffered a congenital birth defect. He had difficulty walking on hard or asphalt surfaces but was fine on carpet or grass.

Within four months the puppies were unrecognizable. Food and care did magic for them. Their eyes cleared, their hair grew, they gained weight, and they each found adoptive homes. Little Toe-Toe, the deformed puppy, found a home with a disabled child with special needs. He's still looking after that young man today. The ringleader of the group, now Willie, lives in the lap of luxury. The other two got great homes with families of their own.

Mike and I adopted or fostered several. We adopted Boomer first and became a part of the rescue volunteer crew. We fostered Molly and Dolly, a mother and daughter pair found wandering an industrial park in Chula Vista nearly starved to death. Molly passed away 11 months later of congestive heart failure. Dolly lived another three years.

We got Ben, who was picked up in the center divider of the freeway near Bakersfield after we lost Boomer to liver disease. We fostered Samantha, who was in the night-drop-off at North San Diego County Humane, flea and tick riddled, starved, and scared to death of people.

We fostered Alpine, another Bakersfield wanderer after we lost Ben to a heart attack. We fostered Sahara, who'd been owner relinquished because of a cross-country move, after three years at the rescue kennel. Samantha and Sahara passed away at 14 years a month apart. Most recently, we took in Piper, an 8-year-old female whose owner has terminal brain cancer. And we would do it all again!

Parts of Speech

Rich Ritter
The New Voice of the American West

NARRATOR (a bespectacled college professor dressed in tweed jacket and speaking in a soothing academic voice, each part of speech enters the room when cued): After another contentious disagreement between Verb and Noun concerning an unexpected shift from transitive to intransitive that left Noun perplexed and humiliated, Noun has convened a meeting of all the parts of speech to resolve the matter. As you can see, Noun is already sitting behind an ornately-carved wood table waiting for the parts of speech to arrive at the small windowless room illuminated by candles. (Narrator gestures around the classroom) A shimmering dress flowing across her graceful legs, feisty Verb is ready for action as she strolls to the front row and sits directly across from Noun. Pronoun, dressed in monotonous gray from head to toe and tired of standing in for Noun (and feeling a bit underappreciated), sits behind Verb and stares at the floor. Wearing colorful but clashing bow tie, shirt, pants, and a dapper porkpie hat, Adjective immediately searches for his best friend Noun when he enters the room, and then saves a seat for Adverb because he knows that she is usually late. Preposition follows closely behind and upon arrival at one of the folding chairs appears confused: should he sit on it or under it? Conjunction, full of youth and verve, but not particularly interested in the meeting or its agenda, skips into the room and quickly glances around so that she knows who is attending or not and then she snuggles next to Pronoun (who she has always admired). Interjection enters with crashing footsteps and a loud exclamation to announce his arrival, but no one pays him a bit of attention because they've all heard it before. Adverb finally appears a few minutes late: she would have made a special effort to arrive on time if Verb or Adjective had called the meeting, but she has never fostered a meaningful relationship with Noun. Shall we listen in as the meeting begins?

NOUN (pounding a varnished wood gavel repeatedly on the top of the wood table): First an announcement: I would like to remind the group that the Articles are attending a jazz festival in the city of New Orleans and do not return until the end of the month. I see that Adverb has finally arrived—late as usual I might add—so let us begin the meeting. Although I asked you all to call me "master" last week, and "Bob" yesterday, please refer to me as "president" today. Better yet, call me "President Bob," if you don't mind. Now, the reason that I—President Bob—have called this meeting, is to—

VERB (her voice quivering with anger, interrupts): What right do you have to call any meeting at all. Just because you are the subject of a sentence and can change your name to Bob, Davenport, toaster, or psychology as you please doesn't give you the right to

91

order the rest of us around. I would like to move that you change your name to "blockhead" or "fool," or better yet, "ignoramus."

Verb turns and addresses the other parts of speech

And furthermore, I would like to point out that he's not the boss of us, even if he decides to change his name to "boss." Who's willing to support me and second the motion?

The other parts of speech sit quietly and do not respond

Anybody? Doesn't anyone in the room have the guts to support me on this? Am I the only one who is willing to take action?

CONJUNCTION (raising her slender arm): I would like to point out that Verb could not have made that motion without my help, and....

PRONOUN (standing and waving his arms): I would like to point out that Verb, bless her heart, used me repeatedly without ever mentioning "Bob" or "president." But as usual, I get no respect for the important role I often play in syntax.

ADJECTIVE (removing the dapper porkpie hat from his exquisite head and using it to gesture): Oh shut up you silly Pronoun. You don't even exist unless the wonderful Noun, which I often modify into something truly wonderful, establishes the primary subject and therefore the primary purpose of the sentence. Without the all-important "Bob" there is no "he" whatsoever. And without magnificent me, sentences would become as dull as a lackluster pronoun.

PRONOUN (speaking to Noun but keeping the corner of his eye on Adjective): Adjective always takes your side of the argument no matter what you say and ignores the rest of us. I don't care what you call yourself. Without me, things would get pretty repetitious around her. Can you imagine? Bob decided to take a walk. On the way Bob met John, and Bob invited John to lunch. As Bob and John continued to the restaurant Bob and John ran into Sally. Bob invited Sally to lunch as well, and Sally accepted. Bob and John and Sally then walked briskly to the restaurant, and when Bob and John and Sally arrived Bob and John and Sally asked the headwaiter, whose name was Fred, for a table near the window. Fred directed

Bob and John and Sally to a table, and then Fred handed menus to Bob and John and Sally, and after a while Bob and John and Sally ordered lunch.

ADVERB (speaking cautiously because she had never developed a direct working relationship with Noun): I frankly disagree. Although he is often flamboyant I genuinely appreciate Adjective and truly enjoy chumming around with the remarkably colorful guy. As a matter of fact, I honestly enjoy hanging around with amazingly supple Verb too, and, not surprisingly, sometimes I even hang around with myself.

NOUN (pounding the gavel on the table again in response to Verb's earlier motion): Look at the mess you've created, Verb! I can't even start the meeting because of your intemperate outburst! I swear, sometimes it's impossible to figure you out. You dart around in the past, present, and future. You change your mood from indicative to imperative at the drop of a hat. You shift from transitive to intransitive and then back again whenever you feel like it. Your voice is never the same, sometimes active and sometimes passive. And don't even get me started on your so-called subjunctive mood. Frankly my dear, working with you is absolutely maddening!

INTERJECTION (finally perking up): Yikes and gadzooks! Did someone say "outburst"? Holy crap!!—that's my job!!!

PREPOSITION (still trying to find a comfortable position under the chair, and then rising and stepping on top of the chair to speak above the din): This whole discussion is flying over my head. If someone doesn't get to the point fast, I'm heading through the door, down the stairs, and across the street to that quaint little pub on the boulevard, the one below that charming bed and breakfast on the second floor.

VERB (the tempo of her words rising): Listen here, President Boob...do you think it's any fun trying to keep up with you? First you're singular, then you're plural, then you're a collective noun, and then you take a coffee break and turn the whole mess over to Pronoun so that you don't have to do any work at all, and I have to conjugate all over again.

NOUN (closing his eyes and shaking his head) The name's Bob—President Bob—and I expect an immediate apology for calling me President Boob.

VERB (rolling her eyes): Read my lips, President Blob. I will not apologize. I have not apologized. I am not apologizing. I will not be apologizing anytime soon.

ADVERB (clapping her hands and smiling broadly): I sincerely love it when she conjugates so remarkably.

NOUN (shaking the gavel at Adverb): Adverb, I can't even remember a single time when you supported me on an issue. You always side with Verb! What is your problem?

CONJUNCTION (surprised and alarmed and speaking to both Noun and Verb): Can't the two of you just work together and come to some sort of agreement and stop all this fighting? After all, can you really write a decent sentence with only a noun or only a verb? I don't think so. I think both of you are important and that you should stop arguing so that we can all go home and relax and enjoy the evening and get on with life.

Pausing to think before continuing

And if you really want a genuine problem to complain about, try the experience of some writer replacing you with a lowly semi-colon in the middle of a compound sentence and then you'll know what true rejection feels like or maybe you won't and this conversation will never end.

ADJECTIVE (waving the crisp, clean porkpie hat in the tense air of the stuffy little room) You think that's bad. How do you think it feels when some thoughtless writer mistakenly uses you to modify a scandalous verb or another glittering adjective? Try that for a mortifying event.

Then turning to Adverb

No intentional offense, my humble friend. You probably feel the same when an insensitive writer uses you to modify a salacious noun, or even a lackluster pronoun.

PRONOUN (he suddenly stands, sniffs, and wipes a tear from his eye): Here we go again. Lackluster pronoun. How come I never get to be the salacious one? Why does everybody always assume that I'm boring? I ask all of you: who ever thinks of me as salacious? Anybody? Any one of you? I would like to be thought of by someone in this room as salacious once in a while. Is that too much for me to expect from any of you?

NOUN (attempting not to snigger): I, your president and leader, would be more sympathetic to your plight if you could ever come up with a decent gender-neutral personal pronoun. The other parts of speech and I, your president, have waited for years.

PRONOUN (his sad expression turning to a sneer): I'm working on it, but every time I throw something out for consideration everyone laughs at me. For example, "shim" was not well received by anybody. Neither was "herm." Frankly, I'm running out of options.

VERB (leaning provocatively against the back of the chair and giggling): Well, you have to admit that both "shim" and "herm" are ridiculous, but not as ridiculous as your earlier attempts. I still remember the unfortunate day you announced "shis." That surprised everyone, including the Articles. One false keystroke by a writer and who knows what kind of trouble she might get into with the editors.

NOUN (standing and pointing the gavel randomly around the room): Enough of gender-neutral personal pronouns. This meeting is turning into a chaotic event. Will someone please make a legitimate motion so that we can achieve a concrete result?

VERB (also standing and waving her arms): Sure, I don't mind taking some action since everyone else appears unwilling to do so. I retract my earlier motion, since you found it so offensive, and move that there is no point to this meeting and that we adjourn posthaste.

ADVERB (aggressively jumping to her feet): I happily second the motion—and what a wonderfully clever use of the adverb "posthaste." Very few writers have properly appreciated that lovely word in my recent memory.

ADJECTIVE (throwing the now rumpled porkpie hat across the room just below the mottled ceiling in need of a fresh coat of pristine paint): And I third the astonishing motion by exquisite Verb. I can see now that I have made a serious mistake by not getting to know this lovely woman better, an unfortunate occurrence that I intend to rectify.

NOUN (his voice shaking and now pointing the gavel directly at Adjective): You can't third a motion, Adjective. And stay away from Verb. The two of you have nothing in common. For starters, look at the clothes you wear. Look at that tie. Look at that shirt. Good grief!

INTERJECTION (exclaiming in a slow crescendo): Did someone say good grief! GOOD GRIEF!!!!

CONJUNCTION (dancing and clapping and smiling): I love it when someone uses "and" at the beginning of a sentence. I wish more writers would do that. It gives me chills.

PREPOSITION (crawling out from under the chair again): Can't we just call an end to this meeting and all head through the door, down the stairs, and across the street to that nice little pub on the boulevard below the bed and breakfast on the second floor? That's my recommendation.

NOUN (slamming the gavel on the table): Order! Order! Get your butts in those folding chairs immediately. Order!

NARRATOR (the parts of speed argue distantly in the background and follow the narrator's cues to leave the room): And so it went for another seven minutes or so, when Preposition, who could not tolerate another moment under the chair, finally took matters into his own hands and headed through the door. And then Conjunction followed, and right behind too. Soon Verb—glad for the opportunity to taunt Noun once again—waved goodbye to Noun with a confrontational flip of her hand and dashed out of the room. Adverb closely followed verb. Adjective ignored the tedious hammering of the ponderous gavel and the chaotic shrieks of Noun and also followed Verb because he wanted to get to know her better (although this is a separate and quite heartrending story of a tragically doomed relationship). Then Interjection yelled several irreverent exclamations, but luckily most of the other parts of speech were out of earshot, and when he had bolted from the room only Noun and Pronoun remained.

Narrator glances first at Noun and then at Pronoun

But our story is not quite finished yet.

NOUN (slumping into his chair and then tossing the gavel onto the table): I give up. There's no way these unruly parts of speech will ever agree on anything. That's it. I just give up.

Pronoun, the only one left in the room, stands and raises his hand

Yes Pronoun, what do you want now?

PRONOUN (glances at his shoes for several seconds before looking up at Noun): I've been considering something.

NOUN (obviously disillusioned with the collapse of the meeting): Yes, yes...get on with it.

PRONOUN (suddenly brightening): What do you think of "heesh?"

Prince or Pauper—Fishing Southwest Alaska is the Ultimate

Evan Swensen

Charlie's pilot made a trip to Southwest Alaska in the old 1948 Stinson Voyager, 857 Charlie. Charlie's pilot's daughter, her friend, and her friend's father completed the party. They flew through scenic Lake Clark Pass and landed at Iliamna. The girls sat in Charlie's swing-back seat, aged with forty years of use. The air through the pass was surprisingly smooth, CAVU weather was wonderful—clear and visibility unlimited. On arrival at the Iliamna airport Charlie entered her downwind leg of the landing approach so that as she dropped her left wing and turned to base her passengers could view their intended Newhalen River fishing site. They could see no other anglers present and they'd have the hole to themselves. Charlie easily landed on the north-south runway, slowing to turn left onto the east-west dirt runway where Charlie parked and was tied down off the edge of the dirt runway between two clumps of brush.

After departing Charlie, their fishing gear was loaded in packs and the two fathers and two daughters took the 45-minute hike to Newhalen River, leaving Charlie tethered by the runway awaiting their return. The river was choked with red salmon. They were stacked like cordwood. It was impossible to bring in a line without a fish on. If they had a hookup and it got off, another took its place. They soon had their limit of six salmon apiece, filleted and packed in packs ready for the hike back to Charlie. The balance of the day was spent in catch-and-release fishing off the rocks for resident fish: rainbow, Dollies, and grayling.

As Charlie's pilot recently fished the Newhalen a flood of pleasant memories flowed across his mind. He remembered his teenage daughter and the fun they had together fishing off the rocks and filleting salmon. Now, 30 years later, Charlie's Pilot's daughter has her own family and fishes and recreates with her husband, daughter, and sons. She also remembers the ride in Charlie through Lake Clark Pass and fishing off the rocks with her dad on the Newhalen River.

On Charlie's Pilot's most recent Newhalen outing he didn't get there in the Charlie the red Stinson, but came in ERA's twin-engine, radar-equipped, instrument-rated, sleek new flying machine. He didn't walk to the river, he went there in a twin-engine, wide-bodied jet boat and fished areas denied father and daughter on their former venture to the Newhalen. There were no daughters on this trip, just Charlie's pilot and captains of industry. Captains who had paid thousands of dollars for their Newhalen fishing experience.

Charlie's pilot was outclassed by his companions with their Ross reels, Cabala's latest outdoor clothing, and gear he'd only read about in the big three outdoor magazines. The equalizer, and his reason for being with the big boys on the Newhalen was his Alaska experience.

Of course they caught their fair share of fish, kept some for lunch and dinner, captured some on film, and released most of them like father and daughter did on the earlier trip to this fishing paradise.

Compared to Charlie's Pilot's earlier trip to Iliamna with his daughter, this was luxury. Nothing was spared. But, comparing memories—walking to the river and fishing off the rocks with his daughter, and to the latest week's angling adventures—prince or pauper expeditions—if he could do either one again, he'd help his daughter into Charlie, fire up Charlie's engine, fly to Iliamna, hike to Newhalen, and fish off the rocks with his daughter.

Publishing My First Book

Adam Freestone
Alaskan Writer of Imaginative Creativity

Writing my first book was difficult. I had to make sure my story and plot were solid and coherent and my punctuation and grammar were correct. Once done, then came the most daunting task of all—getting it published.

Watching numerous videos on the subject gave me an idea of what to expect but none of them gave me the whole picture. This only increased my apprehension because I was probably going to have my book rejected—a lot. I braced myself for this unavoidable disappointment and began my arduous search for a publisher.

While collecting ideas on where to start, a friend heard of what I was doing. He knew a publisher and asked if I wanted to meet them? Thinking this a good place to start, I said yes. I apprehensively waited for the day of the interview, expecting my book would be rejected or I would mess up the interview in some way.

As professionally and confidently as I could appear I participated in the interview. Even if I got rejected, I could learn how to do the next interview better. The interview was going well, until something disastrous happened—the publisher said, my book was too long. After watching so many videos, I knew the simplest mistake during an interview would lead to rejection. Taking a deep breath, I braced myself for the inevitable outcome.

I kept my hopeless hidden and continued through my doomed meeting, answering questions; knowing nothing would come from them. Then when the interview came to a close, something unexpected happened.

The publisher said, "I looked forward to working with you."

I stared dumbstruck as a train wreck of thoughts smashed themselves together inside my head. Statistically, less than 1% of authors get published on their first attempt; it seemed astonishing my luck could have possibly been so good. When I could think coherently, I eagerly agreed—wondering if I was dreaming.

When the publisher left, the only thing I can say was, "did that just happen?" It seemed all the horror stories of publishing were laughably incorrect.

My euphoria however, only lasted until an email came back about my manuscript; it was almost 800 pages! That came as a shock; it was twice the length of anything I had intended to write. My goal was around 400 pages, not something longer than the seventh Harry Potter book!

Fear of rejection struck me and it was due solely to sheer ignorance about how to keep track of book length. I did not consider that there could potentially be such a vast difference on page length when transferring my manuscript to another word processor. I made the mistake of thinking the number of words per page would be almost the same no matter what word processor was being used.

I figured the number of pages would determine about how many words were in the book.

After banging my hand on my desk, (figuratively of course, I actually couldn't do that even if I wanted to) feeling like a moron for getting my book rejected over something so important, I read the rest of the publisher's email. To my surprise, they simply asked me to split the book in half, and then everything would be fine. I breathed a massive sigh of relieve, then groaned at having to break my book up.

It was hard reworking the story I had worked so hard to make. But to my surprise, doing so improved the second half of the story. The split opened many interesting possibilities to explore. So, in the end, I was glad I did it.

Unfortunately, this phase didn't last long. While getting my book ready for printing, I came down with a severe case of pneumonia. One of my lungs had completely filled with fluid. If my condition worsened even slightly, I was in serious danger of suffocation.

Luckily, it didn't, but I had to spend time in ICU. Then due to an insurance issue, I was transferred to another hospital. It was a different hospital but I would still be taken care of. I was sorely mistaken! The hospital I got transferred to was unprepared to care for someone in my condition or situation.

The more likely outcome was I would not live through treatment here. My house was more prepared than the hospital! Despite vigorous protests from the doctors, I left and went home. There, my condition began to improve.

I just didn't get to enjoy improving for long—again. A week after leaving the hospital, the place I live was struck by a 7.9 earthquake. If you've never been through an earthquake approaching this magnitude, imagine the sound of a freight train flying past your head and being tossed violently up and down in your bed, while things are flying off the wall and ceiling. This is worse for someone who cannot dive under a table.

But shortly after the quake ended, an aftershock struck with almost the same strength as the main earthquake. Fortunately, I made it through the aftershock unscathed and without my house sustaining structural damage. Then I find out the hospital I had left days earlier was evacuated. So, if I hadn't decided to leave the hospital, I would have been in it during the quake. It's mind-boggling how many seemingly unrelated things came together to prevent what I almost went through.

Even with my pneumonia improving, after the quake, I struggled with recovering from my sickness for many months. This prevented me from getting my book published. But as soon as I felt good enough to do so, I resumed working toward my goal.

Eventually, I saw the printed form of my book. And considering the hell I endured to get my book printed and all the effort I poured into it; it must be really good.

Race Track or Freeway

Magdel Roets

Writer of Christian Fiction

The driver pulls the visor over his eyes. Secured in his seat, he clicks the car into gear, revs a bit and waits for the signal lights. At the right moment, he releases the clutch and sends a blue smoke up behind his tyres while the engine of his Formula One car screams in its attempt to stay in first place. Leaving the other racers behind, he can go ahead full speed along the open track. There is nothing in his way to stop or distract him.

The writer flips open his laptop, presses the power button and wipes his reading glasses while waiting for the computer to start up.

As soon as the right icon appears, he clicks on word, types a heading, clicks on safe as , clicks save and flexes his fingers. A clear page opens in front of him, nothing in his way, nothing to distract him, full speed ahead, typing his thoughts as fast as his fingers can go.

Lap after lap the racing driver stays in front. Slowly he is closing in on the slowest cars on the track. Just as he is about to pass, the flag waves him in for a pit stop. No use to get annoyed, he has to obey. What a waste of time, as if the scheduled pit stops are not enough. Seconds later he is back on the track, gaining in on the tail of the string of cars in front of him.

The pages fly under the writer's hands; the introduction is finished and the body of the story is starting to show direction. The silence is shattered by a commotion outside, stopping the writer's fingers in mid-air. The sound of metal being dragged over concrete is the cue: the dog has not been fed. This is an unscheduled pit stop for the writer.

On the racetrack things go smoothly for many laps. The driver pass many tail-riders, carefully avoiding collisions, making sure he does not get run off the track by competitors for the title. He drives like a gentleman, but one who is set on winning.

The dog fed, water bowl filled, the writer is back tapping the keys on the keyboard and the characters in the story get to do their thing.

And then it happens. The car in fifth position takes a turn too wide, taps the front wheel of the car in front of him and both spin off the track, colliding, flipping over and sowing metal and plastic all over the track. Yellow flags come out, then the safety car is sent in and traffic slows like on the freeway during peak hour.

For the writer, the scenario equals something like a neighbour ringing the doorbell. The writer opens the door and realises this is not a quick hello, borrow me a cup of sugar and dashing home. The neighbour needs a shoulder to cry on for some yet unknown reason. The characters in the computer are frozen in place until the neighbour has had his say. By then, the writer is distracted, his attention splintered and split between the neighbour's problems, the dog that needs to be taken for a walk, the mail that has to be collected, (this week), and pangs of hunger striking at this very inconvenient moment. This kind of writing is like driving on the freeway at peak hour: go at fifteen miles an hour, stop, go, slowly, stop, mile after mile, breathing exhaust fumes all the way.

While waiting for the debris on the race track to be cleared, the racing driver's thoughts wander to the four hundred mile stretch of open road - with hardly any traffic - from Botswana to Namibia. No competitors, no yellow flags, no unscheduled pit stops, just open road beckoning, and the writer dreams of quiet nights to go on typing until the sun comes up. If only the driver could race along the four hundred mile road at full speed, and the writer could write only when everyone is asleep. But life happens and too often we have to snail along in peak hour traffic until we reach our off ramp where it might or might not get better.

From the reader's point of view it is pretty much the same. The difference is our reason for reading.

My sis-in-law sits down at a table with her book, pen in hand, making notes as she reads. A smile on her lips and a nodding head, she underlines a paragraph. This is good, she is thinking. Five pages on and a frown appears between her eyebrows. No, I absolutely disagree, she says out loud. Going back to read the paragraph again, she frowns harder and makes notes in the margin. I'll have to have a word with the writer about this, she decides. So she putters forth on the freeway, reading, stopping, re-reading, and making progress at the speed of a tortoise at its best. At the end of the book, she has accumulated enough information to win any debate on the topic of the book and has acquired knowledge she stores for future use. Her reason for reading is always to learn something or get revelation on an issue that has been a puzzle for her.

Her best friend, my biggest fan, prefers Formula One reading, but longing for the four hundred mile stretch so she can finish her book in one sitting, going fast and unhindered. I often ask her how she liked the latest book. Thinking hard, she shrugs and says it made her relax and that is all that matters. I ask her what she takes home from reading my books and she replies: "Nothing. I feel good, up-lifted, relieved from stress. What more could you want from reading a book?" Two opposite ways of reading; two opposite reasons for reading, both enjoying reading, one as much as the other.

My wish for all my readers and fans are that they enjoy reading my books. Whatever their reason, whatever their preferred way of reading, as long as they get what they want and have a most pleas-ant experience doing it, I'm as happy as a bookaholic in a book warehouse. To give my readers what they want, I'll keep on writing, whether on the race track or the freeway, as long as I get there and send the next book to the printers.

Red and Blue

Mary Flint

America's Most Promising Science Fiction Writer

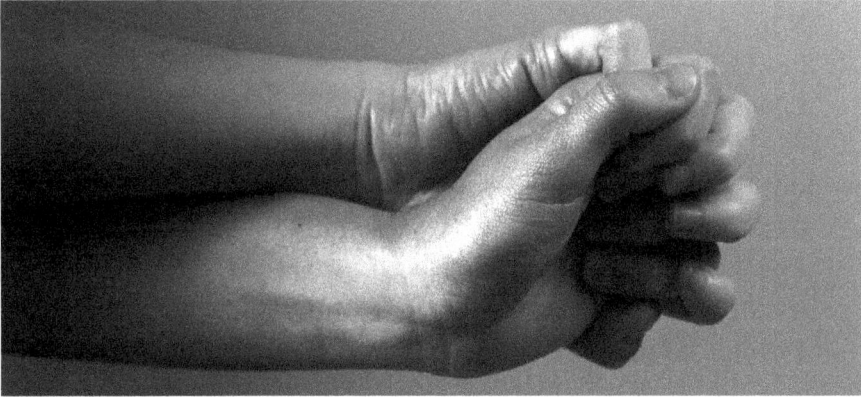

I laid on my back on hard dirt, the remains of a field, explosions and fires erupting around me. I stared at the soot and ash swirling through the sky, falling like black snow from a black sky. The bomb blast had sent me flying, and I must have had a concussion because my vision was fuzzy, and it was hard to think. There wasn't a medic anywhere near me, at least, there hadn't been before the blast, but I had no idea how far I'd been thrown. I couldn't move my arms or legs. Maybe I was just in shock? My eyelids were heavy. Of course I'd be tired after all the fighting. Surely there was nothing wrong with closing my eyes for a moment.

Something blue caught my eye, and I started back awake. I wanted to see what is was. It was difficult with my blurred vision, but I finally figured that the blue was fabric, soiled with soot and mud, and embers had peppered the fabric with tiny holes. It was an enemy uniform, I realized. It wasn't too unlike the uniform I wore. The only difference, really, was that my uniform was red, and his was blue. I had landed beside a fighter from the other team. He didn't look so good. He was starting to fade. I wondered if I was, too.

"Hey, you okay?" My voice was a bit raspy, but I think he heard me. He stirred a little.

"I-I don't know," he called back to me shakily.

"Can you move?" I asked.

"No,"

"Looks like we're in the same way, then."

"I guess so."

We were silent for a moment. Then, the other fighter asked, "I wonder who's winning?"

"Good question," I replied. "I guess we'll find out in a minute."

I saw a spark of light as he began to disappear.

"Do you ever wonder why we're fighting?" he whispered.

I would have shrugged if I could have. "I think I might have once or twice, but it usually makes a glitch."

"I see," the fighter said. "I guess, I just wonder what we win in the end." He looked over at me, his body glowing. "Too bad we weren't on the same team. I think we could have been good friends."

I smiled a little. "Who knows? Maybe we'll be on the same team next time."

He smiled, too. "Maybe. I'd like that."

"What's your name?" I asked. "I'll look for you."

His face went distant. "We don't have names. We're not Mains."

"That's right. My mistake." I gave him a reassuring smile. "See you in the next one, friend."

He nodded, a small smile playing at his lips, then he faded into a cluster of lights that raced up and disappeared in the sky. I sighed, watching my health gauge drain to zero. Oh well. I'd be back in less than a second, and I wouldn't remember any of it. He wouldn't either.

I became a cluster of lights, flying into the sky, then there was only a moment of darkness. Then I was back, my clothes clean, my items and health replenished, back at the Player 1 base. I guess the blue team had won last time, since the battle was starting over.

Other fighters began to leave the base, out into the fray, but I glanced at the fighter next to me. He looked familiar somehow, like perhaps I had seen him before, but wearing blue. But that must have been a glitch, because then I didn't recognize him at all, but I think, if we could ever talk, we would be great friends.

Rin Tin Tin

Valerie Winans
Dog's Best Friend

A blanket of gray covered the earth. It was cold and rainy. Dave looked out the big window—the one I like to look out from the comfort of the top of the sofa—and said, "It's raining cats and dogs." What?

How do people expect us to learn their language when it is so nonsensical. The rain is coming down hard; I can hear it hitting the roof, and I can see it hitting the pavement so hard it bounces back up. I don't like to be outside in a storm. I especially hate thunder and lightening. It's frightening because you never know where or when it will hit. However, I do like to be out occasionally in a light rain. A sprinkle rain sometimes feels good, and then when I come back in the house Val gets a towel and gives me a good rub down. Those rubs feel so good I often try to get back out for a subsequent wetting and rub down. Val won't fall for it, and will insist that I go to my bed, but this day I'm already in my bed having done my daily duties earlier before the rain started, and to top it off —I'm bored.

Val is no fun—she's reading a book. Dave is in his puffy chair pushing buttons and complaining about nothing on the box to entertain him.

I don't usually pay any attention to the box that pulses color and sound, but as Dave was what humans call channel surfing he came to moving pictures without color. This was what probably caused me to look. I also heard the bark of a dog, and I was trying to discern what the dog was saying. He was saying, "Look! Look at me." When I concentrated my sight on him, something very strange happened. Light from the box got very bright and reached out toward me. When the light hit me I began to tingle all over. Every particle of my body was diffused into the light, and I was drawn right into the box!

The first thing I felt was warm; my gosh it's hot here. I looked around and saw that I was in a desert. There were rolling hills and lots of dirt. The sky was clear, and the sun was high. I saw a man that I somehow recognized right away. It was Lee, my friend and trainer. Lee gave me an order, and I complied with his request. We did this many times that afternoon, and each time I did a trick Lee would give me praise. As I was performing tricks for Lee, other men were taking pictures of me. I learned that I had to do each trick to their satisfaction as well as Lee's. Some tricks I did more than once—not because I didn't do it right, but because the men with the camera's didn't get it right. That was alright with me because I had so much fun doing the many tricks Lee taught me, and all the work was worth it when he praised me. I could keep playing these games forever, but soon the fun was over, and we got in Lee's car and went home.

Lee has always been in my life, and he has always taken care of me. My earliest memories are of Lee and my sister Nannette. We lived with soldiers in a camp. Lee was with us, caring for us much of the time. He occasionally would be gone for what seemed to Nannette and I a very long time. When this happened other soldiers would come to feed us and play with us, but there was no one like Lee.

We were always so happy to see Lee when he returned from his work. I think he was happy to see us as well. He would hug us and cuddle us, and play games with us even when we were small. When Lee wasn't working he was with us all of the time. For a time we lived in a barn and he even slept with us. I don't know if Lee was becoming more dog like or if we were becoming more human.

It was Lee who gave us our names. At the time we were born there was a kind of quirky cultural thing going on in France. They made little primitive dolls with painted dots for eyes and mouth. The women would give these dolls to soldiers who pinned them on their gun straps or their uniforms for luck. The male doll was called RinTinTin, and the female doll was Nannette. Thus, I became RinTinTin, and my sister was Nannette.

There was a big celebration in camp one day, and the soldiers were happy because the war was over. Nannette and I didn't know what war meant, but the soldiers were ecstatic that it was over.

Then there came a time when Lee, Nannette, and I got on a very big ship, and although we went up on to the top called a deck several times a day, most of our time was confined in a small space. Nannette got sick, and never really got better. When the ship landed and we got off Nannette went with some other people, and I never saw her again. At the same time Lee got another dog, and he named her Nannette as well. This was confusing to me, because even though I really liked the new Nannette, I never forgot my sister.

The three of us traveled together to a place Lee called California. As far as Nannette and I were concerned our life did not change much. Lee would go away for periods of time to his work, but always provided for us, and when we were together he was continually playing with us and teaching us new things.

Lee took me to a competition where dogs were jumping over a barrier. I had so much fun meeting other dogs, and jumping is great sport. I jumped higher than any of the other dogs, and that made Lee very happy.

Lee was always bragging to people about what Nannette and I could do, but I think I was actually his favorite because he praised me the most. He was so happy when he learned I had been chosen to perform in a movie called Lighthouse by the Sea.

In this story there was an old man and his daughter tending a lighthouse. The old man had gone blind, and his daughter did most of the work keeping the fire in the light going at night. If the authorities found out that the lighthouse keeper was blind, he would lose his job. The daughter was trying to find a helper for them when a man and his dog came to shore from a ship that had been sunk; they hired Albert to help at the lighthouse. (I played Albert's dog in the movie.) Some bad people in the town wanted the light in the lighthouse put out so they could sneak contraband from sea to shore without being seen. It was the age-old story of good versus evil.

They don't make movies by filming the scenes in any kind of order. I jumped from a dingy in one scene and swam for shore, and in another I dug up a stake I was tied to and ran to help the old man—the lighthouse keeper.

I hated the part where they wrapped me in a net and carried me onto a boat. In the movie they also beat up on Albert and locked us both in a room on the boat. I chewed my way out of the net, and then chewed through the ropes tying up Albert.

Albert climbed through a small window about 7 feet off of the floor in order to escape. I could hear him in a battle outside the room, and that window at the top of the wall looked to be the only way out.

It wasn't really the only way out. We were on a movie set, and there were men with camera's pointed at us the whole time. I had to make a couple of runs at the little window to make it look difficult, but there were some toe holds on the wall which made it easier for me to do than it looked.

The hardest trick of the whole movie was running up the lighthouse stairs trailing a long hunk of rags that had fire on the end. In the movie, the bad guys had extinguished the light and tied up Albert. Amazingly, Albert, while tied up, was able to light fire to a strip of rags—with my help of course.

I took hold of the burning rags and ran up the stairs to the top of the lighthouse. Then I had to drop the burning rags into the top of the light to rekindle the fire and illuminate the coastline and the sea. That was some trick. Good thing it was one take because I burned some of my hair on that one.

The most fun was the scene where I fought with another dog. There was no fight to it—we played around for awhile and then I chased him. He made it through a hole in a fence that was too small for me, and got away. I really liked that little bulldog. They tried to make him out to be ferocious, but he didn't have a mean bone in his body. What a good guy he was. The "killer" bulldog and I communicated easily, and we had no intention of hurting each other. We had both done this type of play as puppies. That scene was some of the easiest acting I ever did.

Fighting scenes with humans were more difficult than the play fighting with another dog. Lee and I worked almost every day on that trick. I could bite the clothes, but not the man while trying to make it look like I was biting the man. I could really get into the fight sometimes, but when Lee saw that I was getting too rough he would give me a command to stop. These scenes often took several tries before we could get the picture they wanted.

After we did several movies, Lee and I also traveled from town to town doing personal appearances. I liked this time because Lee and I were together all the time. We were either practicing tricks or performing them on stage. I loved Lee and lived to serve him and receive his praise. Opportunities for both were ever present while we were on the road.

Lee seemed to live for the adoring fans. He never got enough of being famous. Fans of our movies often called me a hero dog. I'm not sure what that means. I do know that people like to put human attributes on animals. If I was a hero it was because in movies I demonstrated for the human race those attributes they most admire. I was loyal, I was brave, courageous, and bold. I demonstrated those behaviors people call heroic in my support for the good. I have often pondered the question of good. What is good?

As I was considering human standards for behavior, I thought I heard a voice that I recognized. I stopped, cocked my head to one side and pricked up my ears. Where is that voice coming from? Is it calling Rinty? No, it's calling something like Remi. I began to tingle all over and a very bright light surrounded me. The next thing I knew I was no longer Rinty. I was Remi once again, looking out the big window from the back of the sofa, and it is good.

Road Trips with Mamaw

Gordon Parker

Tales of Crime and Corruption Creator

When I was very young, I called her Big Momma. She wasn't really big. I was really small.

Later, my cousins and I called her Mamaw. Her name was Blanche. Her nickname was Pigie. I asked more than once how she got that nickname but never got a clear answer.

She was a scion of one of the oldest families in northwest Louisiana's Sabine Parish. She was the strongest personality I have ever encountered. Finding herself alone to raise two young sons just as the Great Depression crippled America, she had to be strong to survive.

She was my grandmother and she had a profound influence on me.

She worked hard every day of her life and saved her money. There was little luxury in her life. Even when something nice came her way, it would more likely be put away for later than used right away. Like the window unit air conditioner my dad and uncle gave her. She turned it on when some of us came to visit. Otherwise it sat silently while her old fans whirled.

Don't even ask about the beautiful, warm beaver slippers my parents sent her from Alaska. After Mamaw left us, we found them under her bed. Still in the original box

She allowed herself two indulgences. Big cars and road trips.

Every five years, our step grandfather, Papaw Rube, would drive her to the Buick dealer in Natchitoches. She would pick out the car she wanted and tell the owner what she would pay. He knew better than to haggle. At least he knew he would sell a car every five years. It was always the biggest, four door sedan Buick made. Papaw would stand silently by, ready to drive her home in their new car.

She refused to fly or get on a ship. Her love of travel was satisfied by cross-country road trips in her big Buick.

Her legendary trips started before the appearance of Holiday Inns or the equivalent. I remember what were called "tourist courts." Small, cheap cabins.

There weren't a lot of restaurants along the roads in those early days. But that wouldn't have mattered.

"We like to eat along the way," Mamaw would say.

She would load her big Buick down with every kind of easily transportable food imaginable. Baloney sandwiches. Cans of Vienna sausages and sardines. Peanut butter.

I've eaten many a sardine sandwich under an oak tree alongside a remote road. I still love sardine sandwiches but no longer need the oak tree or road.

I can see them now enjoying their lunch "along the way." Papaw in his fashionable hat; Mamaw in her shorts. Oh yes. Shorts. At home in those days, she dressed conservatively. But on the road trips, the blue plurale tantum was her uniform of the day.

Sometimes the stash of food in the Buick produced surprises. There was, for instance, the time she presented my uncle's family with a congealed salad she had made and transported all the way to Virginia.

She and Papaw drove the Alaska Highway twice. The second time was for my graduation from East Anchorage High School.

I was going Outside for college after graduation with my own car. I accompanied my grandparents back down the Alaska Highway. That's when I learned my grandmother had a lead foot that would match anything NASCAR had seen up until that time.

One day, after lunch at a roadside diner somewhere in Canada, Mamaw left in their car while Papaw and I settled the bill. We couldn't catch up to her. I was pushing my car well over ninety. There was no sign of her anywhere.

We were beginning to fear she had taken the wrong road. Then we spotted the big Buick at a gas station. I still suspect we might never have caught her had she not run low on fuel.

Mamaw and Papaw have been gone from this Earth for a long time. I like to think they're somewhere in a big Buick with the back seat stacked full of baloney sandwiches, Vienna sausages, sardines, and peanut butter.

And maybe a congealed salad.

Step Out of Your World and Escape

Robin Barefield
Alaska Wilderness Mystery Author

Escaping from your life is the only true way to relax, but escape is not easy in the 21st century. You might be lounging on a beach in Aruba, but I bet your cell phone is keeping your rum punch company on the table next to your chair, and you remind yourself you need to return to your room an hour before dinner to put the finishing touches on the report you've promised your boss. You are enjoying a fun vacation, but you have not escaped.

My husband and I own a small bear-viewing and sportfishing lodge on Kodiak Island in Alaska. Our lodge is located seventy air miles from the town of Kodiak in the heart of the Kodiak National Wildlife Refuge. No roads cross the island, so the only way to reach us is by floatplane or an eight-hour boat ride through rough seas. We don't have cell phone service, and although we do have internet, it is satellite internet with a strict and stingy data limit.

We tell our guests they can use our internet to send and receive e-mails but not for anything else, and please, do not upload or download photos or videos. Turn off the apps and disable location services while you are at our lodge.

Our guests look at us with wide eyes. How could we ask them to disconnect from their lives? How will they survive if they can't watch the news on their phones, follow the twists and turns of the stock market, or catch the latest baseball scores? More importantly, how many YouTube cat videos will they miss during a five-day stay with us?

We often catch a guest cheating at the beginning of her stay when she thinks we won't notice her texting while she holds her phone under the edge of the dining room table. Gradually, though, we see change. The iPhone, held in a death grip when a guest climbed from the floatplane, now only makes appearances after we've returned from our daily adventure. Computer screens that were earlier filled with business documents or e-mails are now occupied by wildlife photos from the day's safari.

The group of six strangers who on the first evening they arrived, barely looked up from their devices to converse, now linger over the dinner table discussing the day's excitement and laughing about the huge Kodiak bear they watched chase a salmon through a small stream.

"I thought he was running straight for Sid," Cathy from Indianapolis says.

"Right," Sid from Melbourne replies. "I nearly needed to change my trousers."

The laughter grows to a roar, and then slowly, the conversation drifts to families and other far-away vacations. No one has glanced at a cellphone in hours.

Guests often tell us their stay with us was the best vacation of their lives. I would like to believe we are completely responsible for their excellent holiday, but I know it's not the truth. They had fun and relaxed because they escaped their lives for a few days.

On day one, our guests ask if we've heard the news of the day. What's happening in the world? By day four, they ask what time the tide will be high and what river we plan to hike the following day. They excitedly tell us about the young buck that walked up to their cabin or the eagle they watched pluck a salmon from the cove in front of our lodge. After only a few days, our guests have unplugged and are beginning to follow the rhythms of our world.

I watch with sadness as our guests wait for the floatplane to take them back to Kodiak and their lives. The chatter dies, and the phones emerge from their hiding places.

I love my job as a guide and naturalist, and I enjoy sharing my world in the Alaska wilderness with others, but I feel our trips are only successful when I see our guests relax. I know if a guest can put down his phone and escape his world for a few days, he will have the best vacation of his life. It's not about us; it's about the escape.

The plane lands, and our departing guests wait for the new flock to disembark before they can load their gear onto the plane. As they pass each other on the dock and exchange pleasantries, one of the departing guests looks at the new arrivals and smirks. "You can put away those phones," he says. "You won't need them here."

Sweet Potatoes, Shrimp, and Understanding Life

Gordon Parker

Tales of Crime and Corruption Creator

Retired Alaska State Trooper Colonel Robert Monk wasn't sure he was comfortable with the conversation.

Monk, a lifelong bachelor, had learned enough about the kitchen to feed himself. He even had a few dishes for which he was well known. He was standing at his stove now stirring one of them. Chunky sweet potato soup. A special request from his younger colleague Leland Fleming. Trudy Fleming stood beside Monk sautéing locally caught spot shrimp heavily spiced with cumin.

Trudy's husband sat at the kitchen table sipping on a peach martini. Another special request, it was a cocktail Monk had learned from his friend Trent Marshall.

Leland Fleming was also a retired Alaska State Trooper Colonel though he was barely fifty years old. He was forced to retire after being diagnosed with a terminal illness. The diagnosis cut short what Monk had thought would be a brilliant career in law enforcement.

"Robert, we're not going to let you get all teary on us," Trudy said. "We've done our crying and we'll do more. But we're going to enjoy as much time together as we have left. And we're going to laugh as much as we can."

"Trudy's right, Robert," Leland agreed. "We're going to live every minute we have left to the fullest. We're going to do everything we want to do while we can still do anything. Who knows? I might even write a book."

"If you write a book, I claim the right to edit," Trudy laughed.

"Granted," Leland responded. "Tonight I wanted to try one of these peach martinis and have some of your sweet potato soup. And spend some time telling lies and talking about old times with you."

Leland took another sip of his martini. He turned slightly serious.

"You know, Robert, we always heard that your life flashes before your eyes as you're dying," he said. "That's true in a way but they don't have it quite right."

Now he had Robert's full attention.

"It doesn't flash by," Leland continued. "It moves by slowly. Day by day. And it's more than just watching it move by. You also develop an understanding of why things happened the way they did. Why you made the mistakes you made."

Leland was silent for a moment.

"When you're moribund, Robert," he continued, "it's comforting, even if you're not forgiven, to at least have an explanation for how you lived your life."

Robert filled bowls with sweet potato soup.

Trudy laid a few sautéed shrimp on top of each bowl.

The three friends ate and told lies and talked about old times and laughed.

Robert Monk's Chunky Sweet Potato Soup with Cumin Shrimp

3 tablespoons olive oil, divided
1/2 onion, chopped
4 cloves minced garlic
2 tablespoons grated ginger
2 sweet potatoes, peeled & cut into bite size pieces
4 cups vegetable broth
Creole seasoning to taste
2 teaspoons Thai curry paste
juice of 1/2 lime
1 pound shrimp, peeled
1 tablespoon cumin
salt to taste

In a Dutch oven or stock pot over medium high heat, sauté the onion in one tablespoon of olive oil until soft.

Add the garlic and ginger. Give the vegetables a quick stir to combine before adding the vegetable stock, lime juice, and sweet potatoes. Season to taste with the Creole seasoning and mix in the curry paste.

Lower the heat to medium and simmer for fifteen to twenty minutes, or until the sweet potatoes are softened.

In a non-stick skillet over medium heat, sauté the shrimp in the remaining olive oil. Season with the cumin and salt to taste.

Ladle the finished soup into bowls. Lay a few shrimp on top of each bowl of soup.

After his friends had left, Monk poured himself another peach martini. He stood in the great room looking out the large window at the magnificent view of Gastineau Channel and Douglas Island.

He thought about old times.

The Christmas Beagle

by Remington Beagle

as told to

Valerie Winans

Dog's Best Friend

My very first Christmas was the best Christmas I ever had because that was when I found my forever home with my humans Dave and Val. One minute I was in a small cage, and the next I was in a big room with lots of humans. Small humans gathered around me petting my ears, and admiring me. There were so many human voices I did not know where to look first, and I was a little bit scared. But when Dave picked me up and held me on his lap I knew I was safe. I fell in love with him right at that moment, and I'm pretty sure the feeling was immediately mutual.

The little people kept asking Dave what my name would be. What's a name I wondered? Dave pointed to the logo on my portable cage and said, "His name is right here on his kennel – his name is Remington." As time went on I learned that when someone said Remington they were talking to me. I learned lots of human words quickly; things like cookie, supper, and leash.

Before Christmas, and coming to live with Dave and Val I lived in a big outdoor kennel with my dog mother and other beagles. My mother always tried to protect me because I was, as she kept telling me, not aggressive enough. We were all fed at the same time, and the bigger dogs would push me away from the food. It got so bad that the man with the food would put me in an area away from the other dogs to ensure I would get enough to eat. The other thing I could not get used to was loud noises. I wanted to get as far away from any loud noise as I could. My mother would find me at the back of the doghouse shivering with fear. She tried to assure me that everything was ok by nuzzling me with her nose and licking my face, but nothing she did seemed to help. The man took me to a big field with other dogs for what he called training, but at the first bang I was back to where we started, and cowering under the truck. I heard him say, "I don't think this guy will ever be a hunter, we need to find him a home as a family pet. I think that's where he will be his best."

That's how I came to live with Dave and Val as what the man called "family pet." Val tells the story that she was looking for a beagle puppy to give to Dave for Christmas, and called a dog breeder in the next town hoping he would have a puppy to sell. He asked her if she was looking for a hunting dog, or a family pet. Val said she definitely wanted a pet. The rest is history.

My life with Dave and Val was much different from the kennel with my mother dog and other dog relations. There were no other dogs at Dave and Val's house. I was all alone. The first night was especially scary. Dave put me in my cage, and shut the door. There was a soft blanket in there for me to lie on, and it was warm in the house (I was used to living outside in a kennel.), but it was so different for me without other dogs to snuggle with that it made me cry. Dave talked to me, but I was so young and did not know much human language at that time. I admit I cried myself to sleep that night.

Daylight brought welcome activity. We went from the kennel outside first thing, and Val thought I was genius for peeing right away. Who doesn't need to go right when they wake up? This natural function not only got verbal praise, but a cookie as well. I could see right away it was not going to take much to please these people. There were many more trips outside with treats. We took some walks, but I was always on a tether. That involved some short runs, and consequent jerk back. I could tell right away that there would be a learning curve with this activity. More important was all the petting, praising, and playing. I wondered how much longer this paradise would last.

Although I no longer had other dogs as companions, Dave and or Val were always with me. I naturally gravitated to their pack. I didn't have to compete with other dogs for food, and there were not any loud noises to scare me. I loved this existence, and constantly looked for ways to please. Val tied a ribbon to a bell, and hung it on the back door. She would take me to the door, lift my paw for me, strike the bell, give me a treat, and then we went outside. It didn't take me long to figure out that if I wanted to go outside I would just ring the bell. Once again, Val thought I was a genius. Oh these humans are so transparently easy to deduce.

My favorite part of any day was playtime in the front yard. Dave or Val would throw a ball for me, or maybe a Frisbee. We were out for playtime one day when another dog appeared at the end of our driveway. This was the biggest dog I had ever seen. He was huge, and black, and very imposing. I growled at him a little, and it must have scared him because he immediately started wagging his short little stub of a tail and gave me body language that meant he wanted to be a friend. I wasn't too sure about it – he was three times my size. He bowed down with his butt in the air; he gave me a friendly bark, and tried to sniff my private parts. I could not resist his savoir faire. Soon we were racing around our yard, sometimes I was in the lead, and sometimes Rudy the Rottweiler took the lead. What an amazing good time we had. The next day I watched out our front window to see if Rudy and his human mom would walk by. Sure enough, there they were! I put up such a fuss Val let me out and it was show time! I had a new best friend.

Val enrolled me in puppy school. What a hoot that was! There were new friends to play with every week, and all kinds of new smells. My spot in the teaching circle of dogs was next to an Alaskan Husky. He was a beauty. I happily competed with him for first in class. Our teacher would often pull either me or my husky friend out to demonstrate whatever she was teaching. One day she was talking about giving more than one command at a time such as sit, then lie down. She pulled me out for demonstration, but she was confusing me. Did she want me to sit or lie? I paused not knowing what to do. My husky friend came to my aid by putting his big fat paw on my back and pushing me into a sitting position. Everyone laughed, and I felt foolish. I gave him a little nip to let him know my frustration as I went back to my place in line. I eventually demonstrated all of the activities in fine form, and after weeks of fun I received my diploma. I now consider myself an intellectual.

Reminiscing about those early days warms the cockles of my heart. I realize that providence brought me to some humans who love me beyond measure, and that many dogs never find the kind of home and love I have – every day has been Christmas for me since that first one so long ago.

It Was The Last Day

Gordon Parker

Tales of Crime and Corruption Creator

On the first day he got the news.

On the second day he climbed high into the mountains. He lay in the spongey moss, letting his eyes soak in the majestic panorama of ocean and mountain that had greeted him each morning of his life.

On the third day, he sat in the great room of his home. He thought of men whose names he had heard mentioned. He conceived a plan.

On the fourth day, he went shopping. There were a few things he needed to make his plan work efficiently.

On the fifth day, he sought the first target. This target did his work at night. Darkness was his friend. This night he didn't know the world had turned over. He who had been the hunter was now the prey. He who was now the hunter watched silently from the shadows.

The moment arrived just after midnight. A pretty young girl, who looked to be perhaps fifteen years old, walked down the dark street alone. He who had been the hunter but was now the prey followed slowly behind her in his pickup truck.

He pulled alongside her, rolled down his window, and spoke to her. The girl shook her head, answering in the negative. She was too slow. The door of the truck opened. A strong hand gripped her arm, pulling her into the vehicle as she struggled vainly to escape.

He who was now the hunter stepped from the shadows, raised the Smith & Wesson subcompact semiautomatic, and fired. The nine-millimeter bullet struck the target at the top of his left humerus where it fit into the scapula, destroying the ingenious ball and socket structure of the human shoulder. He was unable to hold his grip on the girl's arm.

"Run," he who was now the hunter said loudly. Calmly.

The girl ran.

He who was now the prey roared in pain. With his good right arm, he pulled the Mossberg Shockwave twelve-gauge shotgun, known as the "Just in Case," from under the seat. Though it had no stock, only a pistol grip, he was unable to use it with one hand.

He who was now the hunter raised his small handgun again and fired twice more, both rounds striking the former rapist squarely in the forehead.

One man lay bleeding in the pickup truck, his sightless eyes staring at nothing.

The other walked away thinking of the French 75 cocktail he would enjoy before dining on the Rock Cornish game hen he planned to have for dinner.

The cop arrived ten minutes later. He was closest to the scene when the call went out. Even so it took a few minutes to locate the dead man and his truck.

The cop knew the victim. He knew the man's death was not a great loss. He knew there were plenty of people who would like to see the man dead. But vigilante justice was dangerous.

On the sixth day, he who was now the hunter found his target in the parking garage of a large office building. The garage was almost empty. The man kneeling on the concrete, shoulders shaking as he wept, had worked long hours. He who had been the hunter but was now the prey stood behind and over the kneeling man, pressing a Glock semiautomatic to the back of his head.

He who had been the hunter but was now the prey killed for a living. Some he was paid to make quietly disappear. Never to be seen again. With others his employers wanted to send a message. They wanted the killing done publicly and viciously. They wanted to broadcast fear.

Today's killing was one of the latter.

He who was now the hunter could see the assassin's lips moving. He was talking to the man he was about to murder. Telling him why he was going to die.

He who was now the hunter didn't intend to let that happen. He raised the small semiautomatic and fired. His aim was true, breaking the clavical on the would-be killer's right side, shattering the bone connecting the shoulder blade to the sternum. The Glock fell from the fingers of he who was now the prey and clattered onto the concrete.

The unfortunate gunman stared dumbly at his weapon now lying out of reach. He looked toward the sound of the shot, unbelieving. Who would have the nerve to attack him? He killed people. No one killed him.

He who was now the hunter spoke loudly. Calmly.

"Run."

The kneeling man scampered to his feet and ran to his car. He quickly got in, started the engine, and raced out of the garage.

He who was now the prey stood motionless in the garage, his right arm hanging helplessly. He watched as he who was now the hunter raised his weapon again and fired two more shots. Both found their mark.

He who was now the prey lay on the cold concrete. His unseeing eyes remained uselessly open.

He who was now the hunter walked away, thinking again of a French 75. It was, after all, his favorite cocktail. And he pictured the lobster with brandy-orange sauce that was planned for dinner.

The cop arrived on the scene a bit quicker on the sixth day. Still he was not in time to catch he who was now the hunter. Again he knew the victim. Again he thought his death was no great loss. And again the fear of vigilante justice arose.

On the seventh day the man who was now the hunter made no attempt to hide in the shadows. In the middle of the day he walked into the crowd of homeless. He knew he would find his target easily.

Surely, there was he who had been the hunter but was now the prey. In the mind of he who was now the hunter this target was the worst of the bunch. As bad as the other two were, at least they had reasons for what they did. Awful reasons. Unacceptable reasons. Unforgivable reasons. But there was motivation that could be quantified if not understood.

This target did what he did from sheer meanness. There was no other word for it. He was mean.

He who was now the prey was homeless himself. Overweight. Dressed in dirty but serviceable clothing, his dark hair and beard long but somewhat combed, he was working on a much older homeless man. The old man's thin, gray hair and beard were unkempt and matted. He was dressed in rags. His feet were bare. Tattered pants were too short, exposing thin legs. A body emaciated from too much alcohol and drugs. Not enough food.

The younger man, he who was now the prey, was beating the old man mercilessly.

"You held out on me, old man," he who was now the prey said. "You somehow got your hands on ten dollars and didn't turn it over. You'll pay, old man."

He who was now the prey struck the old man again. Again. Again. Blood spurted from the old man's nose. From his mouth. At least one tooth had been knocked out.

He who was now the prey reached down to his pile of belongings and retrieved a long, slightly curved sword. A katana. The classic sword of the Japanese samurai. He spread his legs, holding the sword above his head, stomping his feet in imitation of samurai he had seen in the movies.

He who was now the hunter laughed out loud. So loud that the crowd looked in his direction. The phony samurai heard, too. He turned to look in the same direction.

He who was now the hunter spoke loudly, calmly, as he raised the subcompact handgun.

"You have nothing to fear," he said to the crowd of homeless. "Move away from the fool."

No one had to point out the fool. They all moved away from the man holding the katana. The bloodied old man crawled painfully away

"That little gun won't stop a samurai," he who was now the prey said.

"Perhaps not," he who was now the hunter replied. "But you're no samurai."

He who was now the prey grunted in anger. In a style he thought a samurai should grunt. He stomped a foot as he thought a samurai should

He who was the hunter smiled, raised the small handgun and fired a nine-millimeter round into the lower right leg of he who was now the prey, breaking the tibia. The would-be samurai fell heavily to the ground. He dropped the katana. He who was now the hunter saw a hand reach from the crowd attempting to grasp the weapon.

"Leave it."

The grasping hand disappeared back into the crowd.

He who was now the hunter was finding it difficult to breathe. The simple act of drawing breath had been getting harder as the seven days went by. He knew it wouldn't be long.

He raised his weapon. His arm wavered. He lowered the weapon.

"Your tibia is broken," he observed. "That's a very painful injury. You'll be limping along with difficulty for the rest of your life. Your days of bullying are over. You have made these people live in fear. Now you will live in fear."

The cop arrived on the scene before he who was now the hunter left.

He got out of his car but was careful to keep the vehicle between him and the armed man. He didn't understand why the man was killing these people. It was true they were all bad people. Evil people. But the cop couldn't be sure that it would stop there.

"Drop the weapon, sir," the cop said.

"Sorry, officer," said he who was now the hunter. "Can't do that."

He turned to face the cop.

The cop didn't carry a handgun. He didn't care for them. He did, however, keep the M1, popularly known as the Garand, chambered for a 30.06 and carried by his grandfather in World War II, in his vehicle. During hunting season he used it to bring home moose and caribou. Meat for the winter.

When hunting season ended he left the rifle in his car. He cautiously withdrew it now from the custom scabbard behind the front seat.

"Sorry, officer," came the same reply.

He who was now the hunter took two staggering, stumbling steps forward,

The cop raised the rifle and fired, aiming for the ground in front of he who was now the hunter. The cop saw the dust the bullet raised between the legs of the now physically unstable man.

Much to the cop's surprise, he who was now the hunter fell forward onto his face.

The cop ran toward him. First taking the small semiautomatic from the man's hand, he turned him over.

"There are Rock Cornish game hen and lobster leftovers in the refrigerator," said he who was now the hunter, gasping for air. "Sorry I prepared nothing for this evening."

The cop looked puzzled.

He who was now the hunter smiled.

"It is the last day."

He who was now the hunter took a last breath before closing his eyes.

The Matter of Timber Trickery

Steve Levi
Master Of The Impossible Crime

Captain Noonan, the "Bearded Holmes" of the Sandersonville Police Department, was up to his ears in annual employee assessments. This is not to say he was having a difficult time. In fact, the actual writing would only take a matter of moments – not even minutes. He had an exemplary staff of four and that was as large a staff of detectives as Sandersonville needed. None of them were substandard so there was no need for a painful review of past errors or present shortcomings. He was, to return to his peril, up to his ears in listening to the woes and laments of other officers of the law from up-and-down the Outer Banks as part of the annual Homeland Security conference of preparedness. Everyone – and, in this case, every person – was expected to discuss the shortcomings of their individual departments and what magic administrative cures they were employing. As Noonan had an exemplary staff he had no need of any 'magic administrative cure' for shortcomings he and his staff did not have.

Woe was it that he, in a conference circle of law enforcement professionals who felt exactly as he did about Homeland Security in a geographic setting where the only terrorist activity was double parking on a two-lane road, was next to speak of the 'magic administrative cure' he had employed over the previous dozen months.

However, before it came his turn to dodge and weave, evil became blessed. Just as the captain of another police department began to speak, the tool of Satan began to vibrate in Noonan's cargo pants pocket. There were only two people who had the number of his Beelzebubian device and one of them, the Sandersonville Commissioner of Homeland Security, was present in the room. The other, his wife, was at a bridge tournament. When he slipped the execrable IPhone out of his pocket, the area code on the screen was one he had never seen: 406.

406?

But 406 was good enough for an escape hatch!

Noonan gave a professional, law and order, duty calls look to the Sandersonville Commissioner of Homeland Security who was bird-dogging the meeting and out of the meeting circle Noonan went. He did not stop in the front room, building entrance or parking lot. He was as gone as a grizzly bear in Alaska before the first snowfall.

"Noonan here," he said as he sat in his slant six Dodge Dart whose speedometer had been frozen on 257,965."

"Captain Noonan," the voice was apologetic. "I'm sorry to call but we have a problem here and, well, uh, you are a reputation for solving the odd and unusual."

'I've been lucky," Noonan dug around in his glovebox for a notebook. "Where is 'here?'"

"Ellis, Montana. We are an unusual community. Even for Montana."

"What makes Ellis unusual?"

"We aren't a community the way most Americans view towns. We were formed to provide support for the growing Native American casino industry in Montana. 15 of them. Rather than deal with the rules, regulations and city councils in 15 different communities, the casinos came together and purchased remote property and built the support industries there."

"What do you mean by support industries?"

"Everything casinos would need, from cards and chips to security and the actual cash for payouts."

When the voice said, "actual cash," a loud alarm bell went off in Noonan's brain.

"Cash? What kind of cash are we talking about?"

"Millions. The casinos are required – by Montana law – to have twice as much cash available in the casino as is expected to be gambled. Any one of the casinos can see two, three million a week in gambling and twice that on weekends."

Noonan wrote down "millions!!" in his notebook and underlined it. Then he said, "OK. Now, I need your name. I've got your number."

"Thomas Meagher. Named for my grandfather, the first Governor of Montana."

"OK, Mr. Meagher, are you in law enforcement?"

"Yes. I'm usually called Max. We're a small community and want to stay friendly. I'm the Chief of Police."

"OK, Max. What can I do for you?"

"Tell me why anyone would want to steal 400 pounds of flat toothpicks."

* * *

"Toothpicks?" Noonan mouthed the word as he wrote it out in his notebook.

"Yes, sir, Captain. 400 pounds of them.

"If you're Max, I'm Heinz. I'm only 'captain' when I'm at a crime scene."

"No crime scene yet, Heinz. And, yes, 400 pounds of flat toothpicks."

"Just out of interest, why are you calling me now?"

There was a pause on the electronic link. Then Noonan added, "Just out of interest, no suggestion of impropriety here."

"Well, Heinz. We are a small community with a lot of money – as in cash – in very few places. Usually everyone knows everyone and there are no secrets. Then, suddenly, 400 pounds of flat toothpicks vanish and no one knows diddly. It raises eyebrows, so to speak."

"I can see why you called. Tell you what, let me give you a bunch of questions and I'll work on the theft. Do you have a piece of paper?"

"Yup. Shoot."

"OK, just off the top of my head. Using baby steps, tell me the exact procedure of the transfer of money, the cash, from the bank or vault to the casinos. 15 of them means the money has to go by truck or plane, do I have that right?"

"Airplanes. Small ones because they casino-hop on small landing strips."

"Fine. How many planes are we talking about, how often do they go, how much does the cash weigh in the planes, is the cash recycled in the sense that, say, on Monday morning a lot of cash from the weekend goes back to Ellis? How big is Ellis, how many officers in the police force, how large is the fire department, what are toothpicks used for in Ellis, how do you know they are missing, could they have been misplaced rather than stolen, how many dentists are there in Ellis, how many restaurants in Ellis, can you gamble in Ellis and, and, and, that's all I can think of right now."

"I'll get these answers to you as soon as possible. Do you want some answers now?"

"Nope. All at once. How long will it take to get the answers?"

"Suppose I call you tomorrow about this time?"

Noonan looked up from his pad, through the windshield at the building where the two-day Homeland Security conference was being held. "Tomorrow at this time will be just fine." He paused. "But here's my office phone."

* * * *

History, as Noonan had discovered long ago, was not the story of the past. It was the study of the future. If you wanted to know what was going to happen, all you had to do was read history. This wasn't because history repeats itself, but the same forces for dissembling are never gone. There will always be someone looking for a fast buck, peso, franc or chunk of gold. Humans are the same the world over. There will always be thieves and they never sleep, the reason they have the proverbial 'lean and hungry look.'

When it came to that 'lean and hungry look,' the history of Montana was loaded with far more than its fair share of greed and avarice. Perhaps all would have been well had no gold been discovered in 1860. Thereafter, alas and historically predictable, it was only a matter of time before the Native Americas were forced out and the moneygrubbers moved in. It was a tale as ancient as civilization. There was only one aberration and that was the Battle of Little Big Horn when a United States Cavalry unit was wiped out by a contingent of Indians. Usually it was the other way around.

Ellis, interestingly, was named for Fort Ellis. Or what used to be Fort Ellis. The original Fort Ellis was long gone, of course, but it did leave a bloody legacy. The 2nd Cavalry had been stationed there in the 1870s. The 2nd Cavalry had originally been formed by Andrew Jackson and had fought in the Seminole War and the Mexican American War. Then it was sent into the frontier to protect settlers from Indians in the lands America picked up from Mexico by the Treaty of Guadalupe Hidalgo.

In an oddity of the history of the frontier, in 1857, the 2nd Cavalry was order to fight the Mormons in what would become Utah. The Mormons were resisting federal authority so the Cavalry was ordered to resolve the situation. The Mormons had a long history of being treated both poorly and violently in the eastern states and were not inclined to let the United States tell them what to do in the middle of nowhere. So the Mormons raised an army to fight the Cavalry. Known as the Utah War – as well Buchanan's War and the Mormon War – it lasted less than year.

The best summation of the war was published by the New York Herald on June 19, 1858: "historisized: – Killed, none; wounded, none; fooled, everybody." The only causality, so to speak, was Brigham Young who was replaced as Governor of the territory by Alfred Cummings. In an Executive Action, President Buchanan, gave "a free pardon for the seditions and treasons heretofore by them committed" to any and all Mormons who had participated – or not – in the Mormon Wars.

The 2nd Cavalry did not leave Montana and within a decade was involved with the Marias Massacre in which over 200 Indians, mostly children and elderly Indians, were slaughtered – 2nd Cavalry loses were one killed and one injured – and the Great Sioux War of 1876-1877, best remembered because of the Battle of Little Big Horn.

Just out of historical interest, Noonan pulled up Max Meagher's grandfather: Thomas Francis Meagher. Historically, he was a fascinating character. Born in Ireland he was ardent nationalist who was captured by the British and sentenced to life in prison. Sent to Tasmania, he was able to escape and make his way to the United States. He studied to become a lawyer and then became a solider when the Civil War started. By the end of the war he was brigadier general. After the war, President Andrew Jonson, appointed him as the Montana Territorial Secretary and Acting Governor.

With the suppression of the Indians and the coming of the railroad, Montana became a haven for homesteaders. Not that many, as Noonan noted, because the state had less than a million residents a century later. It was a typical small, agricultural state with the only economic fillip being mining. The Anaconda Copper Company was a powerful economic and political powerhouse in Montana and, perforce, was the focus of union resentment.

The faceoff between the miner's union and the company during the First World War led to a lynching. On August 1, 1917, Industrial Workers of the World labor organizer Frank Little was dragged of his bed in Butte by vigilantes and lynched. The subsequent violence was so profound the National guard had to be called in to quell the disturbance.

The Anaconda Copper Company survived until 1983 when it went under. But the mining frontier in Montana was still profitable. In addition to copper and gold, there was also silver, coal, lead, zinc and manganese. By the turn of the 21st Century, the 'mining' turned from minerals to pockets and purses. Gambling came slowly as long as you were talking about games of chance off Indian reservations. On the reservations, gambling was on steroids. And it was profitable. Noonan counted 15 casinos and none seemed to be having a hard time staying in the black. He also noted they were geographically scattered which, for Montana, made sense as the population was scattered as well. After all, Montana was geographically the fourth largest state, preceded only by Alaska, Texas and California. Three times the size of North Carolina! As Max had told him, clearly there was a need for the supply center to service the scattered casinos. Thus Ellis was created, quite literally, out of thin air.

Because Montana had so few people in large cities, its transportation network was hardly a spider web. There were only two interstates and about 15 highways. Unlike states like Alaska where half the population lived in one city, in Montana there were no cities, just communities. The largest one was Billings at just over 100,000 – a very small city by American standards. The next largest city was Missoula with 67,000 and thereafter Great Falls with 60,000. Bozeman rounded off the top four with 38,000. Compared to North Carolina, Montana was miniscule. North Carolina had more than nine million residents and the largest city, Charlotte, had more than 730,000 of them. The two top cities in North Carolina, Charlotte and Raleigh, had more people than all of Montana.

The history of Montana was similar to that of Alaska, Noonan mused. Both states were vast, remote from the rest of America with few people and no time-honored hard and fast rules of how things ought to be done. Residents solved problems as they came along rather than being consistent. If it worked, everyone did it even though it was a bad idea – in New York. But then again, this Montana where everyone made their own rules – whenever rules had to be made.

Unfortunately for Noonan, Ellis did not have a newspaper. Noonan had always found local newspapers to be a wealth of information for crime fighting. But, understandably, Ellis did not want to publicize its existence.

For good reason.

Next Noonan researched toothpicks. As expected, there wasn't much. Implements for the removal of pieces of food from between the teeth have been around since the cave. But it was only within the past century that toothpicks became an industry. They could be bought almost anywhere and came in a variety of sizes – a fact that Noonan did not know – but were most popular in a round or flat form. They could be purchased in amounts of 100, 250, 500, 1,000, by box, carton or case. If what Max had told him was accurate, 400 pounds of flat toothpicks were into the millions of pieces.

'Toothpicks?' Noonan kept thinking. 'What was the link between toothpicks and some robbery?'

He didn't have even a remote hint to a good answer when Max called back the next afternoon.

"I have to ask," Max began. "Can you tell me why someone would steal more than a million toothpicks?"

"Not a clue so far, but I'm working on it. Hopefully your answers will help."

"Hope so. As to your questions, here's what I've got. The cash we have here in Ellis is in three banks. The money itself is in vaults. The banks do not need to get more cash from the federal government because the casinos simply circulate it. I mean, the banks have enough cash to support all of the casinos even over holidays."

"So cash never leaves the loop of borrowing and returning from the federal government, is that what you mean?" Noonan was scribbling in his notebook.

"Correct. There are no cash deliveries from, say, a federal depository. I'm assuming old paper dollars are replaced at some point, but not on a regular basis."

"OK. Go on."

There was the sound of a ruffling of papers over the line. "The banks were leery about talking about their transfers, which I can understand. Collectively I got what is generally happening. On a predictable schedule, probably every Thursday a certain amount of cash from each bank is put in an armored car and transferred to the airport where it is put in a vault. In the ten years since the operation started, not a single dollar has been missing. And there is a contingent of security personnel in the airplane hangar – different from the armored car security team."

Noonan asked, "Do you know if the money from the bank is actually the bank's money? That is, under most circumstances, when a casino needs cash, it puts in an order. The bank fills the order. The instant the actual cash goes into whatever transportation container is being used, the money is no longer the bank's money. It's the casino's money. So any bank would not know if any money was missing since the responsibility of the bank only extends to the packing of the container."

There was silence from Max for the moment. Then he said, "I don't have an answer for that question. I'm in the law enforcement business, not the banking business. For those of us in blue, what matters is the actual cash. As long as it makes it from Point A to Point B, all is well and good. If even one scrap of paper disappears, someone will file a police report. In ten years I have not seen one police report of any money missing regardless of who owns it."

"True," Noonan added. "But you would only know if the police report was filed in Ellis. If a casino in, say, Missoula ended up short dollars, the casino would file a report with the Missoula police, correct?"

"True, true," Max said. "But you are in North Carolina, right?"

"Yes," Noonan replied.

"Well," Max replied. "This is Montana and we are a small state. There are no secrets here. Every law enforcement agency in the state knows everything about every other law enforcement agency in the state. And, anticipating your next question, even if a casino wanted to keep a robbery quiet, every insurance company would still want a police report. A couple of hundred dollars disappearing in a casino is to be expected. But there's too much paperwork tracking the money for thousands to disappear."

"I see," Noonan said. "Go on with the money."

"OK," Max said as he shuffled the papers on his end of the line. "The transfer facility, that's what we call it, was a lot more forthcoming with information. The cash from the banks is transferred under guard to the facility. At some point after the guards who brought the money to the facility and put the money in the vault are gone. Then another team of team of guards will open the vault and parcel out the cash in crates for each casino. The crates are then locked in the airplanes. The facility has a key to each plane cargo hold and so does the casino. No one else."

"So when the cargo hold is locked, only the casino has the other key."

"Yes. Anticipating your next question, which crates go in which airplane is not consistent. That is, the same planes are not used to deliver the cash to the same casino every week. Not only are the planes scrambled as to location, so are the pilots. As pilots arrive the next morning, Friday, they choose their flight plans from a box at random. No pilot knows ahead of time which plane he will be flying. Takeoff times are scattered as well, but this has more to do with geography than security. The plane delivering cash to the farthest casino leaves first. The cash for the next farthest casino leaves next."

"I think you said earlier there was some hopscotching of planes?"

"Yes, but only for the casinos that are close to Ellis. If the plane is flying across the state to make a delivery, it only makes one stop that day. If, say, three casinos are relatively close to Ellis, yes, the pilots will hopscotch to the three casinos. And again, anticipating your question, the hopscotching schedule is set by the facility, not the pilot."

"Can I assume the same security arrangements are followed by all casinos when the cash arrives."

"The security is the same because the insurance companies require a lockstep procedure. There are guards when the plane lands. The cash is transferred to an armored truck and driven directly to the casino where it placed in a vault."

"Has any armored car been robbed?"

"Nope. Not a one. The armored usually has an escort."

"OK, back to the facility in Ellis. Cash goes into the facility on Thursday but flies out on Friday. What kind of security is there at the facility Thursday night?"

"There's a single guard inside the hangar. There's not a lot he can do because the cash is already locked in the cargo hold of the planes. There are guards around the outside the facility 24/7. But remember, the facility is not just the hangar. It's a transportation hub. This means there is more inside the guarded area than just the airplane hangar. There are two or three warehouses, storage, for everything a casino will need: forks, napkins, maid uniforms, poker chips, card decks."

"Is that where the toothpicks were stolen?"

"Yes. Out of one of the warehouses. It was odd. The toothpicks ordered were round. But somewhere in the process, the round toothpick order was changed to flat toothpicks. When the error was discovered, another order was place for round toothpicks. The flat toothpicks were pushed aside. The transportation cost to send them back was more than the toothpicks cost so they were simply warehoused."

"Then they went missing?"

"Inventory is done every month or so. That's when they knew the toothpicks were gone."

"How did the toothpicks get out of the facility? Is security so lax 400 pounds of something can just disappear?"

"Nope. Security is snakeskin tight. The toothpicks were either taken out piecemeal, say, a box at a time in someone's pocket or they are still somewhere in the facility."

"Wouldn't it be hard to hide 400 pounds of anything in the facility?"

"Not really. If you scattered the crates, you could put them behind other crates and they'd disappear."

"Good point. So, as far as the facility is concerned, there is a single guard inside the hangar and a contingent on the outside. Now, let's take the plane that's going to Missoula. If the casino in Missoula needs cards, maid uniforms or poker chips, are they loaded on the same plane that has to cash that is going to Missoula?"

"No. Planes with cash go with cash. They are loaded on Thursday evening and locked down. If the casino in Missoula needs anything else, it is delivered separately."

"On the same day?"

"Maybe. Those flights are scheduled as needed. Only the cash flights are scrambled by plane, pilot, route and takeoff time."

"And no pilot knows on Friday morning which plane he will be flying or where he is going."

"Correct."

"How about the answers to my other questions?"

"Odd ones, I must admit. Total number of planes flying to casinos with cash is eight. The weight of the cash varies by casino but 800 pounds is the maximum load allowed on the planes by the insurance companies. It's more of a fuel thing than safety. The planes have two pilots each and, say, 400 pounds of cash. That's the max weight."

"Go on."

"Ellis has a police force of seven, six of us on the street. The fire department is full service for a city ten times the size of Ellis. The fire department is large because of the tonnage of casino supplies, we use toothpicks in Ellis to dig food particles out from between our teeth, there are six dentists in Ellis, five restaurants and a dozen what I would call eateries. Can you gamble in Ellis? If you mean do we have a casino, no. If you mean pull tabs and horseracing over the Internet, yes. If you mean high stakes poker games in private residences, I, speaking as the Chief of Police, have absolutely no idea what you are talking about."

"Even in a town as small as Ellis?" Noonan laughed when it he said it.

"If I don't see it, I can't make an arrest."

Noonan chuckled. "Just a couple more questions. I've got a brother-in-law in Alaska who's a bush pilot. That's someone who flies little planes over hundreds of miles of nothing."

"Just like Montana."

"He's told me a lot of stories, some of which I believe."

"Just like Montana."

"He told me the biggest predictable problem with flying was fuel. You could not predict the weather but you had to accurately determine how far you could fly. So you had to have more fuel than was necessary for the trip. You would usually refuel at your destination. No pilot wants to run out of fuel while they were in the air. "

"Seems reasonable."

"But there is a difference between what is happening in Alaska and in Ellis. See, in Alaska, when you fuel plane, it's outside. In Ellis, all of the planes with the cash are in a hangar. If there are going to fly out on Friday morning, those planes have to be ready to fly. They are not going to be fueled before they fly. That's a lot of avgas in a lot of fuel tanks. That's dangerous. I'm assuming there is some kind of super ventilation system in the hangar . . ."

And, that instant, a loud and powerful gong clanged in Noonan's brain.

* * *

Noonan was sitting comfortably in his office and smiling. He was smiling because his tool of Satan was undergoing surgery – his term – for new apps – a term he did not use – and he was thus incommunicado. But only for the moment which, with each passing second, grew smaller. As he was chuckling over his good luck, his administrative assistant, Harriet, came in with a newspaper. It was rolled in a tube and she snarled as she gesticulated the tube toward the ceiling tiles.

"Have you seen what his lordship said yesterday?" Her eyes drifted up. But not to the heavens, just the third floor where the office of his lordship, the Sandersonville Commissioner of Homeland Security, had his throne room.

"Let me guess. Toothpicks and robbery."

"Toothpicks and robbery! How clever you are! I can see your fingerprints all over this story." She jabbed the newspaper tube at him. "Give!"

Noonan smiled. "Let me tell you a story."

"No, I want the skinny on this!"

"It'll take a story. Did you know airplanes get lighter as they fly?"

"What? How is that possible?"

"Because a plane burns fuel. The farther it flies, the more fuel it burns. The more fuel it burns, the less fuel there in onboard. So the plane is lighter."

"Where'd you get that?"

"I have a brother-in-law in Alaska who's a bush pilot."

"So?"

"So, he told me an interesting story once."

"Just once?"

"He's an Alaskan bush pilot and I'm surprised he told me one story that was probably true."

"I'll bite."

"Well, there was a legendary pilot in Alaska by the name of Mudhole Smith."

"Really? Mudhole?!"

"Actually, that was his nickname. His first name was Merle."

"How'd he get the name Mudhole?"

"I'm getting to that. Patience! He was flying out of a mining town a dirt runway that had turned to mud because of the rain. As he was starting to take off, the front wheel of his plane dropped into a pothole and the plane flipped up on its nose. Then the propeller dug a hole in the runway. A mud hole. That's how he got his name."

"And you are telling this because?" She stalled for a moment then shook the newspaper tube at him. "This had better be good and have something to do with toothpicks."

"Sure does. About 30 years after he got his nickname, Mudhole ran a flying operation out of Cordova. That's where my brother-in-law got his start. He started flying for Mudhole."

"OK."

"One day he was clearly overloaded."

"Because the plane was going to get lighter as he flew?"

"I presume so. Anyway, my brother-in-law struggled – and he told me he struggled with agony in his voice – to get the plane off the ground. He said the plane didn't fly; it lumbered. I'm guessing when a bush pilot says the plane lumbered, it was a bear to fly."

"OK."

"When he got back, Mudhole was furious."

"Because the plane was overloaded?"

"Naw. Mudhole yelled at him, 'You had another 500 feet of runway! You could have loaded on another 100 pounds of cargo!'"

"No!"

"Yes!"

"What does this story have to do with toothpicks?"

Noonan tapped the newspaper roll with the forefinger of his right hand. "The key to the robbery his holiness supposedly foiled was weight."

"Weight? Toothpicks?"

"Correct. Everyone was focused on the toothpicks as theft. The thieves knew what they were doing. This was an inside job. And it was well planned. Well ahead of the robbery, someone jiggled the order of toothpicks. They needed flat toothpicks, not round ones. So someone changed the order of round toothpicks for flat ones. When the flat toothpicks came in, someone, probably the inside person, noticed the alleged mistake and reordered the round toothpicks. It was too expensive to send the flat toothpicks back so they were just mothballed. Then they were forgotten."

"Except for the thieves."

"Yes. The thieves took the cartons of flat toothpicks and hid them around in the warehouse. The toothpicks never left the warehouse."

"Why use them at all?"

"Weight, Harriet, weight. That was the key to the entire operation. Somehow the guard inside the hangar could figure out which planes were going to which casino. Maybe by the number of crates of cash aboard. As soon as the planes were loaded with cash on Thursday evening he was locked in for the night. The keys to the individual cargo hold in each plane were in the hangar so he would have had no problem opening any cargo hold. The hangar has a massive ventilation system because there are so many airplanes loaded with avgas. The perps outside tapped into the ventilation system and dumped in the flat toothpicks. Inside the hangar, the guard made sure the toothpicks were blasted into the cargo hold of the plane that was going to be robbed. They had eight hours to get the 400 pounds of toothpicks into the plane. When the cargo hold of the plane was loaded with the 400 pounds of toothpicks, the ventilation system was put back in order."

"So the plane was overloaded. Wouldn't the pilots know that?"

"No way they could have known. The cargo hold was locked. They just got in the plane and flew. They expected to have enough fuel for the trip but came up short."

"Because of the extra weight."

"Yup. The thieves knew what they were doing. They put enough weight into the plane to force it to run short. Running low on fuel is not unexpected. Usually it is because of weather. The plane was too heavy for the fuel it would have had normally so the plane had to make a landing for more fuel. That's where the thieves were waiting."

Harriet wiggled the newspaper. "And that's where they were caught. Clever!"

"Crime doesn't pay."

"Sure it does," Harriet said she jabbed the newspaper roll – again – at the ceiling tiles. "His lordship is making the big bucks up on the third floor and we're down here."

"You can always work on third floor."

"Not a chance! Doing nothing is hard. And you never know when you're done."

The Mind of a Villain

Rich Ritter

The New Voice of the American West

Before an inexplicable chill of nostalgia erupted from beneath his skull and shuddered down the core of his spine to his sweaty lumbar, Csongor Toth reminisced of his childhood as an impoverished peasant frolicking in the pastoral lands of eastern Hungary—although he did not appreciate the vigor of his peasantry nor the depth of his poverty until the eventful years of adolescence.

He recalled his father sitting on a shabby chair with three wobbly legs and telling colorful stories of the great Hungarian Revolution. The event had played out in 1848, three years after Csongor's birth, and consequently meant little to him.

He remembered a dreary vision of his mother stumbling across a plowed stretch of dark ground on a bright spring morning with a large bag strapped over her shoulder, but he could not recollect the cheerless expression on her face or the pointless contents of the bag.

He remembered his infatuation, at the age of 14, with a flirtatious peasant girl, his elder by three years, and he recalled with delicious clarity the savagely-prurient dreams that began emerging from the murky subliminal folds of his pubescent mind following the night she spurned him.

He remembered the days after his sixteenth birthday when the startling epiphany erupted into his thoughts that his unfortunate birth into an impoverished peasant family was an absurd cosmic error demanding immediate rectification. He recalled his promise to take whatever actions were necessary to remedy the error. He subsequently made plans to procure the wealth necessary to finance both travel to a larger city and a suitable female tutor who could provide for his education and play a central role in his increasingly ravenous dreams.

He remembered the night he entered the home of the wealthy family, only a few miles away from the disgusting little hovel his own family had lived in from the time before his birth. He did not originally intend to take anyone's life, but after emptying a box of jewelry and precious coins rather noisily, his discovery by the father had left him no other choice. After using his fists to beat the poor gentleman nearly unconscious, he had employed a length of curtain cord as a garrote to finish the job.

It was regrettable that he had wandered into the man's bedroom across the hallway, because he was thereby obligated to asphyxiate the man's deliciously plump wife with her own nightgown—an act that had required equal measures of dexterity and strength. But in both instances he had experienced a curious surge of euphoria, which he later discovered could not be recreated in any other way— although the euphoria soon faded and usually vanished altogether within a day.

He discovered the children, a boy and a girl, in separate rooms at the end of the hallway. He decided to let them sleep after experiencing a fleeting twinge of conscience (this surprised and amused him at the time).

He remembered the primal urge to look up the peasant girl who had rejected him a few years earlier. After several inquiries he learned of her unfortunate demise from cholera. He recalled weeks of depression following the discovery of this wasted opportunity. He eventually recovered from his emotional muddle and began his journey to Budapest.

He soon found living quarters appropriate to his recently improved financial status. He placed an advertisement in the newspaper for a female tutor with expertise in philosophy, languages, and mathematics. After interviewing six highly-qualified but rather unattractive applicants, a woman in her twenties who possessed the requisite intellect and presentation arrived on his doorstep in desperate need of a job. (It turned out that she was also on the run from an avaricious suitor and needed a place to hide, but this little nicety was not revealed during the interview.)

Csongor had hired the young lady on the spot with the understanding that she would tutor only him and that she would teach him something new every day—unless some dramatic personal calamity allowed the possibility of a day off.

He remembered his sacred pledge to control the full expression of his salacious appetites until he had achieved mastery of mathematics, English, German, and philosophy. Regrettably, he fell somewhat short of this promise on a rainy Friday afternoon during a contentious debate on Immanuel Kant's notions of ethics.

Although the exquisite rapture temporarily assuaged the tiresome consequences of this untidy business—another newspaper advertisement, more interviews with disagreeable women, arduous negotiations over petty details, and, of course, the inconvenience of....

The Night Ed Almost Shot Me

Evan Swensen

Ed and I were hunting from a lodge located on a lake at the base of Mt. Susitna. The lodge, in its first year of operation catered to hunter clients from Germany. I was invited by lodge management to check the place out in hopes Alaska Outdoors would send them clients, both German and domestic. I ask Ed if he'd like to join me. He consented and packed his bags.

Upon arrival at the lodge, via floatplane, we were welcomed by lodge personnel and introduced to other guests including a hunter from Germany I'll call Otto. Otto wanted to shoot a moose or black bear; animals he could take without securing the services of a big game guide. He was wearing the best and latest outdoor clothing, which appeared to have been recently purchased from the German equivalent of Cabela's. His hunting gear reflected the same newness and top of the line, expensive equipment and accessories. He looked like a walking advertising page from a hunting gear catalog. He was hunting alone and decided he would tag along with us; which was all right.

The morning of the first day of the hunt dawned bright, clear, and chilly. Hunting protocol from the lodge dictated hiking from the lodge or taking a canoe to various parts of the lake. We decided on the canoe. Lodge workers were helpful in getting the canoe ready and supplied us with life jackets, food, and whatever we were expected to need for the day.

Otto placed his food in his high tech back pack, hung his brand new, super duper, state of the art binoculars around his neck, and slipped the sling of his beautifully, polished rifle over his shoulder and walked to the dock. The young man from the lodge held the canoe for us expecting that we knew how to safely get on board. While Ed and I donned our life jackets Otto proceeded to be the first to get into the canoe. He seemed to be in rush to get into the middle seat, perhaps having discovered that there were two paddles and obviously, the person in the back and front would do all the paddling. Otto did not wait for instructions or assistance—he just stepped onboard; quickly discovering the instability of the little craft.

Ed and I completed our life jacket putting on just as Otto stepped into the canoe. Of course the canoe quickly overturned and Otto entered the lake with a huge splash. The water was armpit deep as Otto became vertical. There he stood holding his binoculars and rifle high above his head with water dripping from the scope, rifle, and binoculars. Obviously, his lunch and every other thing he was carrying and wearing was socked. Ed and I did all we could do not to laugh.

For Otto, the day was ruined. He declined our offers to wait for him until he changed and regrouped. I admit that we laughed out loud as we witnessed Otto slogging and slushing across the dock and up the path to the lodge. Ed and I were careful as we boarded the up righted and dried out canoe.

At the end of the lake Ed and I discovered a path leading into the woods. We decided to follow it. It led past an old, but sturdy cabin and wandered off into what looked like prime hunting country—which proved correct. Near the cabin and in various places where we walked we were required to step around or over bear scat—some still steaming in the cool morning air.

We soon found ourselves surrounded by moose; mostly cows. However, there was one huge bull standing among the cows. His position in the herd did not allow for a shot. Ed slipped one direction and I another hoping the bull would separate him self from the cows and give one of us a clear shot. In just a few minutes the moose wandered off keeping the cows between the bull and me. As they walked into an open place the bull stopped and raised his antlered head high as the cows moved on. It was a perfect headshot. I took careful, steady aim and pulled the trigger. To my surprise the moose didn't drop but scurried away into the brush unseen by Ed.

You may imagine my embarrassment and disappointment at missing. Ed was kind and helped me make ego saving excuses. As we thought about it we both decided that perhaps before we continued the hunt we should check the gun's accuracy. We shot a few times and found that the scope was off by a long ways. It must have been jarred in the plane or canoe, or dropped by the pilot, dock boy, or lodge people. Anyway, my ego was saved, the rifle sighted in again, and the hunt continued. And the hunt became just a hike as the shooting had scared all the moose out of the area.

Ed and I decided, rather than to return to the lodge, we'd stay in the old cabin for the night and we could get up early and hunt again. It was a good plan. It was a little disconcerting as we again walked over and around bear scat as we made our way back to the cabin.

The cabin was a nice place to stay and we had a pleasant diner and went to bed. There was some talk about bears and what we would do if we had any trouble. Independently, we decided to keep our rifles close just in case.

During the night I needed to go to the bathroom and slipped out the door of the cabin. Ed did not wake up. As I came back in the door made a noise, which brought Ed upright clutching his rifle and bolting a shell. In the dark I heard the guns action and could feel Ed's concern—maybe panic.

I know that I was near panic as I yelled, "Ed, it's me; don't shoot." I don't know how close Ed was to pulling the trigger. I just know it was the night Ed almost shot me.

The Perfection of Imperfection

Mary Flint America's

Most Promising Science Fiction Writer

As a classically trained musician, I spend hours a day learning and practicing a piece of music with the ultimate goal of reaching perfection. But what, the question could be asked, is this "perfection?" Some may say it is the complete and whole repetition of what is written on the pages of the piece, not a wrong note sounded, every dynamic and marking followed completely and without mistake. The instructions, often written with words such as "adagio" or "allegro," to dictate the tempo, or how fast or slow the music should be played, must be followed without deviation. But I ask, is this perfection what gives music its ethereal beauty?

My answer?

No.

To play a piece perfectly as I have described would certainly be beautiful, intense, gentle, or whatever instruction is noted on the score. But this is not why I, as a musician, strive for perfection. Because speaking frankly, never playing a single wrong note hardly ever happens for me, even with hundreds of hours of practice behind my performances.

Yes, the music would be technically correct if every instruction indicated on the score were followed exactly, but everyone who performed a piece would always perform it the same way. It would be correct, but would it be perfect? All we have to dictate how the piece should sound is what is written on the page, but we will never know how Beethoven played his Pathetique Sonata, or how Bach played his Toccata and Fugue.. Perfection for those pieces would be how they sounded in the mind of the composer when they were written, but that is music only they could hear.

Even with modern composers who have recorded their own works for us to listen to, perfection could only be achieved in replicating exactly every detail in the recording, assuming the composers even liked them. I'm sure they made mistakes when they performed as well. How could we, the audience, know if the recordings are, in fact, perfect?

Not even instruments are the same. Two violins may look alike in every detail, perfect you could say, but their sounds would be different. Perhaps not noticeably so, but every instrument has a different voice, just like a person. As if it was hard enough to achieve perfection already, one would have to also find the exact instrument the composer wanted when they wrote the piece.

So, is this perfection? Would music performed in such a manner be able to reach people's hearts and touch and inspire their souls?

No. Only beauty can do that.

Beauty, I believe, comes from the emotions, stories, and experiences that are poured into the notes. The reason I strive for "perfection," per se, is so that I do not hinder the beauty I am trying to portray in the music. I have to know the piece I am playing well enough to play it smoothly from beginning to end. Only then do I have an opportunity to create music. The audience will not be able to read my mind. They will not know where the sadness, happiness, or anger that is portrayed in the music comes from, but that is not the point. I am providing them with the means to imagine where they come from. That is what makes a musician. That is what turns music into art. The ability to bring the audience into the music.

Perhaps there will be a wrong note along the way, but if it does not hinder the beauty of the music, it is still perfect.

Writing is no different. As writers, we can see our stories almost, or even as vividly as what we see with our physical eyes. But we only have words to describe the scenes we see before us. Readers, no matter how eloquent the writing, will always see something differently than the writer, whether it is the scenery, or a character. We could memorize an entire thesaurus, but we will still have only words to convey such a massive and vivid image. Even poetry and philosophy are interpreted differently by different people.

But that isn't the point.

Words, written with elegance and prose, allow the reader to enter into the stories and visions we as authors so vividly see, and allow them to experience it for themselves, and perhaps even heal a broken heart, or bring hope to the discouraged. Our job as writers is to use words, like musicians use notes, to allow our audiences into our stories, worlds, and minds, to travel miles without taking a single step.

That to me, is true, imperfect, perfection.

The Road Less Traveled

Rebecca Wetzler
Purposeful overcomer sharing the fruit of faith

The phrase The Road Less Traveled originated in 1916 from Robert Frost's poem *The Road Not Taken,* using the last stanza:

> Two roads diverged in a yellow wood,
> And sorry I could not travel both
> And be one traveler, long I stood
> And looked down one as far as I could
>
> To where it bent in the undergrowth;
> Then took the other, as just as fair
> And having perhaps the better claim,
> Because it was grassy and wanted wear;

Though as for that, the passing there
Had worn them really about the same,
And both that morning equally lay
In leaves no step had trodden black

Oh, I kept the first for another day!
Yet knowing how way leads on to way,
I doubted if I should ever come back.
I shall be telling this with a sigh

Somewhere ages and ages hence:
Two roads diverged in a wood, and I
I took the one less traveled by,
And that has made all the difference.

The simple reason Robert Frost wrote the poem was to poke fun at a dear friend of his, Edward Thomas, a frequent walking companion. Thomas would choose their route, yet invariably grouse that they probably should have taken another path. However, when Edward received the poem, he totally misunderstood its meaning as being about serious reflection on decisive action.

Frost was disappointed his joke was missed, but later admitted it was a tricky poem, knowing it was thought-provoking with dichotomous application. Subsequently, two schools of thought developed for what he meant by 'I took the one less traveled by, and that has made all the difference.'

The more popular thought for choosing the path less traveled was it ultimately made a positive difference in his life despite its challenges. However, the second interpretation is that, though at first the paths seem different, upon closer inspection the fact was time 'Had worn them really about the same.' Therefore, given the choice of which road to take was not clear, perhaps the point of the poem is that there will always be a lingering wonder and possible regret for 'The Road Not Taken.' What is clear, however, is that choices are required, and they make all the difference.

For many readers the imagery of crossroads in nature evokes spiritual metaphors for meditative decision making at the crossroads of life. Robert Frost himself never made his spiritual beliefs clear, which has caused much speculation about what he was communicating in his works since spiritual elements are found in some of his writings, and he talked about God with others, contemplated the possibilities of His existence.

His mother raised him in the Swedenborgian church, also known as New Christians, which is considered a cult by most Christian denominations. Its central belief is that God is one person in Jesus Christ, rather than the biblical Trinity of three in one: God the Father, God the Son and God the Holy Spirit.

Did Frost follow his mother's faith? Or was he agnostic, though he contemplated it, explored it, he did not commit to any spirituality? Regardless, his mastery of literary expression with its lyrical rhythms, ambiguous depths, and psychological complexities inspire his readers to commune with their spirits, exploring for hidden meanings.

Other writers were inspired by the phrase and the premise that choosing the road less traveled made a more positive difference in life. The most notable was Dr. Scott Peck, a psychiatrist and self-professed Christian Mystic. His book *The Road Less Traveled: A New Psychology of Love, Traditional Values and Spiritual Growth* (originally entitled *The Psychology of Spiritual Growth*), along with his subsequent similarly-themed books, have become classics associated with the New Age Movement (which emerged in the 1970s), though he did not label himself as such. Rather he was a Buddhist at the time of writing the book in 1978, followed by in 1980 he claimed conversion to Christianity. However, though his version of spirituality used legitimate biblical theology, he retained eastern religion beliefs including pantheistic monism, meaning God is all things, all things are one and given we are one with God, then we are god, and will recognize this as we advance in our spiritual growth.

Peck's eclectic approach resonated so well with millions because he stated right out that 'Life is difficult,' but then proceeded to offer the solution to life's mental and spiritual problems was to embrace the pain of problems because therein lay the meaning of life. He presented great insight into the human psyche with practical advice on self-discipline, problem-solving, caring for others, and fulfilling one's own potential.

His spiritual growth theology then deviated from Christian doctrine by melding spiritual enlightenment with attaining mental health stasis via encouraging readers to 'transcend' traditional culture mores. This teaching fed in well with New Age spiritual pluralism, which supported the misdirection that saving oneself is found in being conscious of the god within one's own moral consciousness regardless of religion, rather than the traditional belief that salvation is found only through accepting the literal sacrifice of God's Only Son Jesus Christ for our biblically defined sins, saving our souls for eternity.

When it was originally published in 1978, Peck's book would have been considered the road less traveled given the New Age movement was in its infancy. In more recent times, 2011, another writer was inspired to title his memoir simply *The Road Less Traveled*. It is a lesser known book written by Charles E. Cravey, a 39-year pastoral veteran of the United Methodist Church. He said the book was his attempt at 'putting an exclamation point' to his life, a life he has found to be a collection of precious and special experiences—experiences he had because he took the road less traveled and is living a life serving others through Christian ministry. Through the years he was inspired to write a treasure trove of poetry mixed with short stories encompassing family memories, unforgettable mission trips, ministerial undertakings, emotive eulogies, scriptural lessons, and biblical instructions he compiled into a devotional representing life lessons learned.

Though he did not explicitly refer to Frost's poem, Reverend Cravey utilized phrases from it in his book demonstrating his familiarity with it. Based on his work, readers are presented the traditional Christian culture mores anchored in biblical truths, in contrast to Peck's work. By the time Reverend Cravey's book was published, the New Age Movement was well entrenched in our society, having enjoyed decades of growth with its attractive self-centeredness yet inclusive diversity, untethered by traditional dogmas. In accepting individually defined morality, which will not lead to a utopian anarchy such diversity envisions, the movement helped deteriorate the necessary societal structure provided by the very fundamental spiritual beliefs it opposed.

Adhering to biblical truths is indeed the road less traveled, as evidenced in these familiar scriptures. Matthew 7:13-14 talks about entering the narrow gate, for wide is the gate that leads to destruction. Proverbs 14:12 warns that a way may seem right to man, but it may lead to death. Then one of my favorite verses, Isaiah 30:21, says 'Whether you turn to the right or to the left, your ears will hear a voice behind you saying, "This is the way, walk [ye] in it."'

We must listen with discernment to hear His voice and obey His instruction. However, mankind is innately independent; God gave us free will to believe and do what we want. Subsequently, our initial nature is to not like being told what to do, especially by an unseen authority speaking through an ancient text, the Bible, which has centuries of controversy about whether it really is the inherent Word of God, should He actually exist in the first place. Faith makes belief and obedience possible.

It is interesting to note that according to a 2011 *HuffPost* blog post by Howard Steven Friedman, statistics indicate the four largest religions have millions or billions of followers: Christianity 2.3 billion, Muslim-Islam 1.5 billion, Hindu 900 million, and Buddhist 400 million (the Non-religious/atheist population was estimated at 1.0 billion). Based on these statistics, Christianity seems to be the *Road Most Traveled*. It depends on how a person defines their own individual faith in Christ, though, that determines whether they are on the biblically prescribed *Road Less Traveled*.

I embrace the interpretation that Christianity is a devoted relationship, not just professing belief in a certain religion. My relationship with Christ is foremost in my life, integral to my identity, whereas basic religion is a set of rules to be followed, and it may or may not matter if there are consequences for breaking them.

We all know about the Ten Commandments, and the harsh punishments meted out in the Old Testament days if not obeyed. Nowadays few of them are legally punishable, pretty much only Do Not Steal and Do Not Kill. The rest have been relegated to good character traits: honoring God (consisting of having no other gods, no idols, not take His Name in vain, keeping the Sabbath holy), honoring parents, faithfulness to vows, truthfulness, and being content with one's own lot in life.

In the New Testament Jesus basically re-stated the Ten Commandments into two, which are found in Matthew 22:36-40. Jesus tells the disciples the Greatest Commandment is to love the Lord your God with all your heart, soul, and mind; and the second is to love others as yourself. These spiritual truths are not religiously universal, they exist only in Christianity. Loving God and loving others involves subordinating our own wants and desires, even needs, to serve God and our fellow man. We need to seek His will before we make decisions, or risk heading down the wrong path in life.

By studying His Word, praying for His guidance, and daily inviting His presence into our lives, we will follow the path He has set before us, even if it appears dark and difficult. As we live what we believe, others will see how our faith overcomes adversity and keeps us returning to peace that passes understanding. And though there may be a time when we nostalgically think of the seemingly easier road not chosen, we realize by following God's lead we truly did chose the better path, and it has made all the difference.

Joshua 24:15 "But if serving the LORD seems undesirable to you, then choose for yourselves this day whom you will serve, whether the gods your ancestors served beyond the Euphrates, or the gods of the Amorites, in whose land you are living. But as for me and my household, we will serve the LORD."

The Tale of Grady Dellaneaux

Mary Ann Poll

America's Lady of Supernatural Thrillers

Grady Dellaneaux strode up the pebbled walk leading to his half million-dollar home. He pulled his coat collar close around his neck, trying in vain to protect himself against the frigid mist carried in on a dense fog.

"Stupid weather!" he exclaimed.

The weather wasn't what ate at Grady. In fact, he liked bad weather. It always lifted his spirits. What devoured his emotions this evening was the news he'd been delivered.

"I'm sorry, Grady, but we've had one too many complaints from our clients," Mikale Frandlong, the owner of Frandlong and Associates CPAs said.

Frandlong held a sandwich in one hand and the phone receiver in the other while he delivered the crushing news.

"I expect you to be gone by the end of the day."

Grady turned to leave—no run—from Frandlong's office.

"And, Grady, you may want to get an attorney. Arthur Longdon is threatening a lawsuit. Seems he thinks you skimmed quite a bit of his money last quarter."

Grady turned and looked Frandlong in the eye. "Nonsense! I told him as much when he accused me yesterday."

Grady narrowed his eyes and shook his head. "See where being loyal got me? I knew better! Ten years down the tubes. Thrown out without a second thought. Just like the wrapper on old Frandlong's sandwich."

Grady smirked. *If old Frandlong only knew how much I have taken in ten years. I slipped up with Longdon. I'll take care of him tomorrow.*

"You are condemned to hell, Graduate Dellaneaux."

Grady spun on his heel and squinted into the dense fog. No one there. The sickening-sweet, Southern voice of his long-dead grandmother continued to echo through Grady's brain.

He grabbed his head with both hands and whispered vehemently, "Shut up, old biddy. I tried it your way. Look where your morals got me! I'm doing it my way now, thank you very much!"

A familiar and cold terror tore at his stomach and whispered into his mind, *What if the voices are back?*

"I won't allow it!" Grady answered.

Rubbing his temples, Grady recited under his breath, "You aren't real, you aren't real, you aren't real," until the pressure in his head subsided.

Grady let out a slow breath and continued up the short flight of steps. He inserted the house key into the bright brass dead bolt glistening in the pale-white streetlight.

"I've been waiting for you."

Grady tensed, gripped the key between his index finger and thumb and slowly removed it from the lock. He turned, holding the key waist high and squinted at the dark figure in the shadows of his white-columned porch.

"It's you," Grady growled. He dropped his hand to his side. "What are you doing here at this time of night? You scared the ghost right out of me."

A tall, lean man stepped into the light. Donald Renphrow held out a manila envelope.

"You left instructions to have this package delivered post haste. If the instructions were wrong I'll leave, and you can come by and get it when the shop opens."

"No, no! I'll take it now." Grady reached out greedily.

The visitor stood motionless.

Grady's mouth tightened. He forced his voice to be calm. "I really have a lot to do tomorrow, and it is late. Please give me the package."

After what seemed an eternity to Grady, Donald Renphrow held the package toward him.

Grady seized it. "Thank you," he mumbled, hurried into the house and shut the door. He listened for Renphrow to leave.

The entry clock ticked loudly in the otherwise silent house. Grady strained to hear above the clock's noise.

The sound of heavy boots going down the steps, then steadily growing more and more faint was music to Grady's ears.

Grady double-checked the lock, placed his keys in their gold tray on the foyer table and hurried over the marbled entry to his personal study. He peered to either side to ensure he was alone, walked in, closed and locked the door.

He ripped open the package and smiled as he pulled out a leather-bound book. Reported to be 200 years old, the book showed signs of having been a deep crimson in its early days but now was splotched by black, like new blood mixed with old. He set aside a note and a small round ampule filled with amber liquid.

"*The Book of Fallen Angels*," he whispered and gently stroked the worn leather as if it were a newfound love.

After several minutes he remembered the note, picked it up and read:

Congratulations. As you know, you were the top bidder for this book. I commend your determination. It is rumored that whoever owns this book has unlimited access to the powers of Lucifer and his army of fallen angels. With this text, you begin a journey from which there can be no return. It does not come without price. The liquid accompanying this note is the catalyst for the change you must make if you hope to understand and access the powers of this book....

"What a lot of hooey," Grady snorted. He threw the note aside and stared straight ahead like a stubborn child refusing his broccoli. His brow furrowed in thought.

What if the note is true? What if I can only access the book's power by drinking this stuff?

He picked up the vial and held it to the desk lamp. He tipped it backwards, then forward, contemplating the oily brown liquid as it coated the sides before melting into itself. He removed the stopper and inhaled cautiously; an unknown but pleasant odor.

"What could it hurt?" he asked. He returned to the note.

...It will be unpleasant and probably painful. You must be and stay alone during the process. It could take several hours for the transformation to be complete...

Grady Dellaneaux did not care about physical pain. Being a small and thin child, he was a favorite whipping post for school bullies and others in his youth.

He could not, however, tolerate waiting. Grady opened the right-hand drawer of his office desk and pulled out a syringe.

He stared at the needle left from his grandmother's last days when her only pain relief came from frequent morphine injections.

"I knew this would come in handy someday." He opened the hypodermic and the vial. His ears throbbed with his rising heartbeat.

He placed the thin spike in the amber liquid and watched the fluid slowly rise up the plunger. When it was full, he pushed the stopper until a small amount squirted from the tip. He rolled up his left sleeve and inserted the needle into his vein. He waited.

His skin tingled. His throat went dry. Excited, Grady jumped up and rushed to the mirror in the foyer. A slight built, balding man stared back.

His reflection revealed a slate gray tone to his skin and a navy-blue hue creeping around his lips.

His quickening pulse slowed and bounded at the same time. Grady felt power with every beat. The room began to spin and his arms and legs went numb. Grady Dellaneaux fell to the floor, welcoming whatever would come next.

He lay there listening to the entry clock chime one, then two, looking forward to the next stage of his transformation.

Grady smiled. "I will finally have my revenge and my reward."

"You will have your reward alright. You are condemned to hell, Graduate Dellaneaux."

The sickening-sweet, Southern voice was no longer in his head.

Grady rolled his eyes toward the voice.

His grandmother looked down on him, eyes blazing with judgment, wagging her finger in his face.

"You were hell, old woman," he mumbled.

"You made your own life horrible!"

As he watched in horror, her foot lowered to his chest, twisting and crushing it like an old cigarette butt. The pain radiated to every joint in his body.

Mercifully, Grady went numb again; a powerful calm overtook him. He smiled triumphantly at his grandmother.

"You can't hurt me anymore. I am more powerful than you now."

"It is not I who you should be concerned with." Grandmother Dellaneaux pointed to the ceiling.

Grady looked up.

A triangle of three large, scaled beings crawled above him. Their bloated arms, legs and torsos reminded Grady of marshmallows. Their swollen bodies shimmered with an iridescent grey light, keeping them slightly out of focus. Long, anteater snouts protruded from small, malformed heads. Their mouths were open in a permanent O. The leader inhaled.

The air left the room. Grady gasped in short, fast breaths seeking any oxygen he could.

"You see, when you bought *The Book of Fallen Angels,* you sealed your fate. Did you truly believe you could summon demons and subject them to your will?"

"Others have."

"No, Graduate, others have not. Your need for power and wealth made you easy prey for a great deception."

"You are as crazy in death as in life, old woman."

She ignored him and continued, "It is a risk to obtain a prize sought after by those even more evil than you. This book will be back on the market in a few days. Donald Renphrow will see to it. You always did trust the wrong people. Mr. Renphrow knew you'd do anything to achieve complete power. It was easy for him to dupe you into poisoning yourself."

"You lie!"

"Do I? You're the one talking to a ghost."

The large, pale beings catapulted off the ceiling and joined Grady's grandmother.

"These are your fate. You now serve those you sought to control."

Without warning, the calm numbness gave way to a roaring wave of pain. Grady's whole being shouted for relief. It did not come.

He opened his mouth in a silent scream. Grady arched his back, lifted his arms and called forth his body's remaining strength. He reached for his grandmother's throat.

She stayed just out of range, watching in amusement, her eyes pulling him to her until there was nothing else in Grady's line of sight.

The demons moved in on Grady.

"You are dead, Graduate Dellaneaux," were the last words Grady Dellaneaux ever heard.

The Time Travel App

Cil Gregoire
Alaska Si-Fi Queen

Nearly everyone agreed the new time travel app was the greatest invention since the internet. True, the new app had its limitations. It wasn't time travel like in the Vids. The user could only go back in time, not forward. Also no one was going to travel to the distant past to see who built Stonehenge. A time traveler can only travel as far back as the support system for the time travel app has been in place. Right now that's a year, but as time moves on, the app will work further back in time.

Still the time travel app has proved to be very handy. Are you late for a life changing appointment or an important transport connection? The time travel app can transport you back in time, to be on time. Did you say or do something you will always regret? Finally, you can go back and this time get it right. It is worth the pricey cost of time travel to straighten out your life.

"But wouldn't that be changing the future?" reporters asked when the app was introduced.

Adam Suko knows more about the time travel app than anyone. He invented it. "Physicists don't have the answer to that question yet," Suko admitted. "There is not enough collected data to make a determination. Some theorists argue that when changes occur, the time line simply splits and both realities continue to exist."

"But what about safety? What safety precautions are in place?" the media demanded to know. "Does this open us up to terrorism?"

"There is nothing to fear," Suko reassured the people. "Users of the app must submit to a complete 3-D scan including a mind read before the app can be activated. No one harboring nefarious intentions will be able to get through."

"But what about privacy? Isn't a mind read scan an invasion of a citizen's right to privacy?"

"Sometimes we have to surrender a little privacy in order to enjoy technological advances and still stay safe."

Despite all the concerns, the new time travel app became an instant success and at age 27 Adam Suko became a world hero. But Adam was unsatisfied with his great achievement.

Why can't I move forward in time? The system is in place now and will be then. To solve that mystery he would have to first succeed in bringing a time traveler, traveling to the past, back to the present. Adam's obsession to solve the equation robbed him of all enjoyment of his great fame and fortune.

Adam Suko became the app's most frequent user. When he couldn't solve the problem in the present, he traveled back in time to the system's start up, before the app became available, and tried to solve it from there.

For months he labored over the project, barely eating or sleeping, but all to no avail. When the release date of the time travel app approached the challenge remained unsolved. Frustrated Adam considered dropping the app all together, but feared unknown consequences.

So Adam traveled back to the beginning to try again. He failed again and tried again, repeating this pattern for the remainder of his life. Adam Suko died at the young age of forty-nine, three months before the time travel app was released.

Truth and Lies

Mary Ann Poll
America's Lady of Supernatural Thrillers

Once there were two men, Truth and Lies. They both professed love for a woman named Wisdom and both asked for her hand in marriage.

Lies said to Wisdom, "You are the most desirable woman in the world. You can have anyone your heart desires. Yet only I can give you all the earth's treasures and more. Choose me!"

Truth listened to Lies, looked to Wisdom and smiled. "You are indeed the most sought-after prize on this earth. I cannot offer you what Lies can. I can only promise to seek your counsel before I act on any decision, never forget you are in my life and to treat you as the rare jewel you are."

Wisdom turned kind eyes from Lies to Truth. She said, "You both have much to offer. I must consider before I make my decision."

Wisdom retreated to her sanctuary.

Lies spat, "What have you to offer Wisdom? You are ridiculed, ignored by humans, all but extinct. You are ugly and poor."

Truth turned his earnest eyes on Lies and smiled.

Lies continued, "I have been called an angel of light. I can deceive even the smartest human being. I have destroyed royalty, holy men, judges and peasants. I have put them to death while they begged to live forever."

Truth replied, "All you say appears correct. Yet you have destroyed no one. They chose to follow your false promises—a decision which led to their ruin. You do not have the power to put even a blade of grass to death."

"Even so, Wisdom would be a fool to choose you."

"Wisdom is never a fool," Truth replied.

"No sane woman would choose you, Truth. Your way is one of hardship and ridicule. People would sneer at her because she chose the way of Truth instead of the way of this world.

"No, Wisdom will choose me. I can offer her comfort. She will never want for anything in this life. In return, I will have Wisdom and rule this world."

"We shall see, Lies. We shall see."

Wisdom returned. "I have considered both of your arguments."

She took Lies hands in hers and said, "You have been with me for more years than Truth. And I have been loyal to you. You have courted me relentlessly. You have promised me freedom from financial worries. You have offered me all I can imagine or think of in this world which would give me an abundant life. I cannot understand why I've held back my affections from you."

"I knew you would choose me! Tell Truth to leave!" Lies said.

Wisdom held up her hand. She turned to Truth. "You offer me a life of trials with no guarantees for happiness. You offer me a life of challenge and possible danger. Yet you offer me more than Lies has in all of these years."

"What? How?" Lies demanded.

"Truth has offered me life. He will tell me when I am making a decision leading to my downfall instead of my growth. He will give me strength to make the right decision when I am tempted by lies to take the easy way out. He will help me to continue to be a pure example to others. He has given me purpose and a partnership. So, Lies, I choose Truth."

"So be it—for now. I will be back to ask again after you've gone through need and pain. Then, we shall see who you choose!"

Truth said to Lies, "Wisdom has made her choice. You see, Lies, Wisdom has always been mine; without her I am nothing and without me she is only a lie."

We All Leave Footprints

Robin Barefield
Alaska Wilderness Mystery Author

I work in the wilderness tourism business, an industry described by many names, including adventure tourism, green tourism, and sustainable tourism. Ecotourism is my least favorite of the tags applied to my line of work.

Please don't misunderstand. I believe when you work in the wilderness, you must run a clean operation and impact the environment, the wildlife, the native plants, and the local people as little as possible. We try to do everything we can in our operation to minimize our impact and leave no trace. Ecotourism, though, is a label which has become synonymous with "environmentally beneficial." A guest who books a stay at an ecotourism lodge often believes she is staying someplace where she will not impact the environment at all. After spending most of my life running our lodge with my husband and working as a wilderness guide, I believe it is impossible to walk into the woods without leaving a trace and making an impact. The real problem occurs when a guide labels his business as ecotourism either because he thinks it is so clean it makes no impact, or because he understands the label will attract more clients.

I don't believe many businesses in the United States can accurately be labeled ecotourism because the term has a lengthy, specific definition, and to be an ecotourism business, you must meet each criterion of the meaning. One of the stipulations an ecotourism business must follow is to invest money in environmental and cultural programs sponsored by the government. Countries like Costa Rica actively support and work with ecotourism lodges. The U.S. government does not.

Definitions aside, though, how can we become better stewards of our environment if we believe we do nothing wrong? When we hike up a stream with our guests to watch bears, and we accidentally spook a sow with two small cubs, causing them to run off into the woods, we make sure our guests know we scared the bears, and we have no way to measure our impact on them. We're not perfect. We do the best we can, but we leave footprints in the woods.

The following story describes our worst day of bear viewing in the last 35 years. It was a day we likely killed three bears. This event impacted my life forever, and I never forget I am an unwelcome visitor when I step into the Kodiak wilderness. The best I can do is walk softly and stay no longer than necessary.

This tragic tale occurred in the mid-1980s during our summer bear-viewing trips when my husband, Mike, and I were walking down the beach with five guests. We had finished bear viewing for the day, and since there were no bears in sight, we talked quietly among ourselves. Mike heard a noise and looked up on the hill above the beach where he saw a sow watching us. He immediately knew the bear was more than curious; she was agitated. She popped her teeth, and foam frothed from her mouth. Mike yelled at us to move back, and although I had never been frightened around bears, the sound of his voice made my legs tremble. I repeated his orders to our guests, who were trying to understand the situation.

Mike yelled at the sow again and then pumped a shell into the chamber of the .375 H&H rifle he carries on our bear-viewing trips. Usually, the loud, metallic sound of injecting a shell into the chamber of the rifle is enough to deter curious bears, but it did not affect this bear. She stomped her front feet on the bank and lunged from side to side, while she continued to foam at the mouth. Mike fired once into the dirt in front of her, a maneuver sure to make her flee. She stood still for only a moment and then flew down the cliff straight toward Mike. He shot again, and she dropped six feet from him.

At the time, I didn't realize what an impact those few seconds would have on the rest of my life. All I felt then was grief and sympathy for the sow's two yearling cubs. Mike was so distraught over the experience, he considered never taking another bear viewer into the woods, but he knew brown bears rarely charge humans, and this probably never would happen to us again.

The following day, Mike skinned the bear and turned the hide over to the Alaska Department of Fish and Game. From examining one of her teeth, a biologist determined the sow was 23 years old. Both the biologist and Mike believed with her advanced age, her senses might have been impaired. She was probably asleep, and when she awoke and heard us walking down the beach, she considered us an immediate threat to her cubs and didn't hesitate to charge.

The biologist gave the cubs a 50% chance of surviving through the winter. Not only would they have to avoid being killed by larger bears, but also they'd need to build up their fat reserves, find or dig a den, and live through hibernation without the aid of their mother.

For many years after the sow charged us, I dreaded our bear viewing trips, and I was wary of sows and cubs. Looking back, I now believe I suffered from post-traumatic stress disorder, and it took a long time to overcome the trauma of that sunny, July afternoon. The experience heightened my respect for the speed and power of Kodiak bears, and it was also a crash course in understanding the differences between a bluff charge, often seen with sub-adult bears, and the real thing.

I no longer worry about getting close to brown bears. On the contrary, I love sitting on a riverbank watching bears chase salmon, and seeing a sow interact with her cubs is a special treat, but after the tragic July encounter so many years ago, I will never again be complacent around brown bears. I know I leave footprints when I walk in the woods.

We Are Not Alone

Cil Gregoire
Alaska Si-Fi Queen

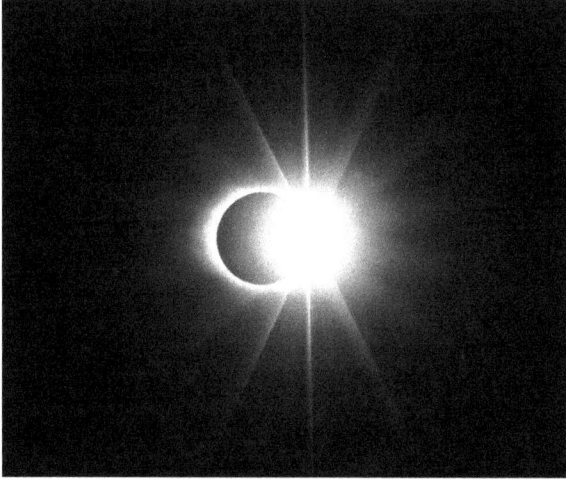

An interstellar space freighter picked up an unidentifiable signal during a return trip to home base. "What do you think it is?" the captain asked her crew.

"There is no response to our greeting, Captain. Sensors do not detect life," her first mate reported.

Deciding to investigate, the freighter intercepts a small-unmanned spacecraft that appears to be of alien origin. The freighter approaches the unidentified object with caution.

Upon closer inspection the captain and her crew are further convinced the craft came from another solar system and offered definitive proof that we are not alone in the universe. With a cargo bay mostly empty, the captain decides to latch on to the foreign object and take it on board. Signaling ahead about their find, the news becomes an instant media sensation.

Upon docking at the orbiting space station, the freighter is instantly taken into custody. A team of government officials accompanied by armed guards takes over the ship.

"What is the meaning of this?" the furious captain demanded.

"Your cargo has been confiscated," the official informed the captain.

"My cargo is not your property. I hold savage rights."

"You will inform the media that your claims of finding proof of intelligent alien life was all a hoax. Then you are never to speak of it again."

"Are you telling me, the government intends keeping a find like this secret?" the captain bellowed in rage.

"If you or anyone on your crew disputes the government findings that this was a media hoax, you will quickly find yourself in jail," the official stated coldly. The armed guards accompanying him left no room for argument.

The confiscated alien spacecraft is taken to a secret area on the planet's surface where a small select group of linguists and scientists study it in secret isolation. Where did it come from? What was its purpose? What did the hieroglyphics and recordings mean?

The linguists determined that the recordings aboard the spacecraft represented not one, but several different languages. Some of the sounds and images were disturbing. The scientists searched for the spacecraft's point of origin based on collected data and determined the alien civilization posed an impending threat. Further study and analysis were needed. Meanwhile, the public must be protected from learning there is other intelligent life in the galaxy. Not even the world leader can be told of the secret conclave due to plausible deniability.

46,000 years has passed on Earth since Voyager 1 left to explore our solar system. The little spacecraft traveled 19.2 light years across the void of space before reaching the heliosphere of another solar system. Gathering solar energy once again it resumed its transmissions to Earth including images of its own capture by the space freighter. The transmission will reach Earth in about twenty Earth-years.

What Makes Americans America

Victoria Hardesty
Author of Action, Adventure and Suspense with Arabian Horses

Did you ever wonder why Americans are the way they are? Could it be the spirit of the original immigrants to this continent who came here with their two hands, few tools, and managed to carve a civilization out of what had been a wilderness? Those original settlers left the land that birthed them for the freedom to worship their deity in the manner they chose and were willing to risk everything to do it. Could some of that spirit have survived in us?

I believe it has. Examples of that are in the news every day and have been for more than 200 years.

Think about how the founders of our country sat down and agreed as a body to fight a monarch with the finest army in the world to keep their freedom. They were a rag-tag band of farmers, merchants, and laborers who picked up their guns and fought for the freedom to choose how they lived and who governed them.

Think about how many young men joined the army in 1915 to fight oppression in Europe and how many of them gave their lives for people they didn't know.

Think about how many young men joined the army in 1940 to fight a dictator who was exterminating millions of people because of their religious beliefs.

Move forward to today. There was a recent article about a group of people on a beach in Florida who saw two swimmers in trouble with rip tides. People on the beach formed a human chain and pulled those two swimmers out of the water to safety even though the beaches were posted "No Swimming" because of the danger of rip tides. They did not know the swimmers, but they were willing to risk their own lives to save them.

Think of the ranchers in Iowa who pulled together a caravan of hay for the farmers in Nebraska they never met when the floods in Nebraska drowned crops and herds of livestock were dying of starvation.

Think of the men from a small church in a little town near me who got together with their Pastor and flew, at their own expense, to Georgia to help rebuild what tornadoes tore apart. They didn't know the people affected, but they were willing to help them because they needed help.

I remember caravans of feed and equipment pulled together in California and driven to Texas by volunteers to help people they didn't know with their livestock after a hurricane.

Every day, when a traffic accident happens, people who don't know those affected will stop their cars and get out to aid and comfort the injured until law enforcement, and paramedics get there.

This is what we do. This is what we are. We come in all colors, all creeds, and we help those who can't help themselves, even risking our own lives to save someone we've never met.

I'm proud to be an American!

What Makes Writing Beautiful

By Rich Ritter: The New Voice of the American West

An idea, a thought, an image dwells within;
Hidden among the murky folds of conscious thought;
Yearning to play within another's mind;
But captive to the limits of expression.
The question is, "How does one break these bonds?";
And connect the two dissimilar minds as one;
Though perfect connection is not possible;
Because each mind knows only of itself.
Write a symphony: quite impractical for me;
Learn to paint: not interested in that;
Write a novel: I think this is the answer;
To link our minds in a beautiful embrace.

Why Do We Celebrate Easter?

Rebecca Wetzler: Purposeful overcomer
sharing the fruit of faith

The quick answer does not do justice to the complex significance of the Crucifixion and Resurrection of Jesus Christ. Let's examine important elements of this religious holiday.

- When did sacrifice become necessary? From the beginning, God gave man the freedom of choice. However, if Satan had never aspired to be higher than God, he would not have tempted Eve, and she and Adam would have innocently chosen to obey God and lived happily ever after in the Garden of Eden. Being naïve, however, Adam and Eve did not understand the consequences of disobedience until they ate of the Tree of Knowledge; once they did, they understood right from wrong, felt shame, leading them to cover themselves with leaves, inadequately, and hide from God. Of course, we can't hide from God, He is omnipresent, omniscient, omnipotent. To provide adequate clothing, God sacrificed animals and made garments for them. And thus began the need for the covering of sin. While we know sacrifice existed from this beginning, clear instructions are not documented in the Bible until Moses took the Israelites out of Egypt. Leviticus 17:11 says "For the life of the flesh is in the blood, and I have given it for you on the altar to make atonement for your souls, for it is the blood that makes atonement by the life." Additionally, once the very specific rules were established, only the tribe of Levi were allowed to submit sacrifices to the Lord on behalf of all the tribes. Further, the Israelites were God's chosen people, all other nations subject to His judgment had an unclear path to salvation. Not so once Christ came, as he was the final sacrificial Lamb. The most beloved of all scriptures, John 3:16 tells us "For God so loved the world, that he gave his only begotten Son, that whosoever believeth in him should not perish, but have everlasting life," and Galatians 3:28 further clarifies, "There is neither Jew nor Gentile, neither slave nor free, nor is there male and female, for you are all one in Christ Jesus."

- Understanding the need for Christ's sacrifice, what is the origin of the word 'Easter?' One theory is it is a derivative from an obscure pagan Anglo-Saxon goddess of spring named Eostre. This assumption is based on writings of an English monk born in the late 7th century, the Venerable Bede, where he said the early Christians were celebrating the resurrection of Christ in Eosturmonath, the Old English word for 'Month of Eostre,' which is April. But that does not mean that Easter is based on a pagan ritual, rather it was common for the early Christians to replace pagan customs with pertinent religious ones. Reverence of Eostre has been revived by polytheistic neopaganism, filling out her mythological story with characteristics of other spring goddesses and elements of Easter celebrations. Another theory is that the word 'Easter' comes from an older German word Ost for 'east,' which came from an older Latin word for 'dawn.' The inference being Spring dawns anew from the east.

- Why is Easter sometimes in March and sometimes in April? Some pagan and religious customs alike are related to the rotation of the earth rather than to a specific day on the calendar. Pagan religions celebrate the spring equinox for renewal of life, giving thanks to their many gods of nature. Depending on the exact alignment of the sun and the earth, the spring equinox occurs on March 19th, 20th or 21st. In the Bible God gave very specific instructions for Jewish feasts and celebrations, also some related to seasons. The Passover is probably the most important Jewish Holiday. It celebrates the Jews escaping their bondage in Egypt, the name being based on the 10th plague God put upon Pharaoh for not letting His people go, the death of all first-born. God told the Israelites to sacrifice a lamb for each household, placing its blood upon the doorpost so death would pass over their homes whereas it would take the first-born in the Egyptian homes not so marked. In Exodus the people are instructed to annually celebrate the Passover for 7 days, starting the 15th day of Nisan (using the Hebrew calendar), which coincides with the first full moon after the Spring equinox. The Passover is important to Easter because Jesus was in Jerusalem for the Passover when he was arrested and crucified; with the narratives in the New Testament describing the events, we know the crucifixion was on Friday, and the Resurrection was on the following Sunday. Therefore, Easter is on the first Sunday following the first full moon after the Spring equinox. Jesus was the ultimate Passover Lamb; accepting and believing His sacrifice covers an individual's soul with His blood, so God's judgment will pass over the person with sins forgiven. Therefore, His resurrection conquered death for all time.

- Where did the bunnies and eggs come from? While there is anecdotal reference in the Eostre myth regarding hares and eggs, there is disagreement if there is sufficient ancient evidence for it or if the elements were orally added as time went on. More than one mythology story used both motifs to represent rebirth and fertility associated with spring. Hares and rabbits began appearing in Christian art during the Middle Ages, although the reason for their inclusion is still obscure. Possibly because of the inference of fertility and virginity, as it was a common belief at the time that hares were hermaphrodites and therefore representative of the Virgin Mary. As for eggs, they were not eaten during Lent, when many Christians observe Jesus' 40 days in the desert by fasting meat and its byproducts. The early church would boil the eggs rather than letting them go to waste. They may be colored red to represent the blood of Christ. The first reference to the hare, or bunny, being associated with colored eggs did not appear until the end of the medieval age, in German Protestant folklore. Children were told if they were well-behaved, a bunny would leave them colored eggs. As the story evolved, children made baskets for the bunny to leave the eggs in, bringing the well-known symbols of today together in one story.

- How important is it to believe the Easter story? Now none of this is very relevant if the Easter story did not really happen. A non-believer may think religion is just to explain the unknown or to provide a social structure. For a believer, evidence of God (Father, Son and Holy Ghost) is everywhere. Two examples:

1. Think of the calendar. In the ancient world, dates were based on important events and/or careful chronologies of rulers. The Roman calendar under Julius Caesar was organized somewhat differently for counting days of the year; then in 523-525 AD a papal chancellor ordered a monk named Dionysius Exiguus to calculate the date of Easter, and instead of using the current emperor's reign as the basis for year, to use the birth of Christ. This method of counting years became the basis for our modern calendar. Therefore, Jesus is the linchpin for expressing the passage of time. For hundreds and hundreds of years the abbreviations BC, Before Christ, and AD, Anno Domini, which means 'the year of our Lord,' have been used to identify the before and after Christ's birth. Unfamiliar, the abbreviations CE, Common Era, and BCE, Before Common Era, have been showing up recently in writings instead? Upon research, changing the semantics is apparently to remove the religious implications in deference to non-Christians... however, changing semantics does not change the fact that Jesus' life is the basis for how the world counts the years. Additionally, people have erroneously guessed CE means Christian Era and BCE is Before Christian Era, so trying to disassociate from the Lord does not make it so.

2. Go back further than the calendar, think the beginning of time. Easy for believers – Genesis 1:1 "In the beginning God created the heaven and the earth," Intelligent Design. For non-believers – the Big Bang. Which according to

brilliant scientists such as Albert Einstein and Stephen Hawking, using the theories of general relativity and quantum mechanics, was an initial singularity of infinite density containing all mass and spacetime of the Universe in a very limited point that exploded and has been advancing out across space for billions of years. The explanation gets more confusing from there unless you are a brilliant scientist. It was interesting to note that some physicists are not sure singularities exist, or rather that current knowledge is insufficient to explain infinite density, before time and space existed.

Which one is harder to believe? God, the Intelligent Designer created everything, or Infinite Density chaotically blew it into being from nothing. There is no doubt man's knowledge has exploded in the past hundred or so years, that the understanding of the sciences, of physics, is impressive and much is provable through hard work and experimentation. It comes down to what Hebrews 11:3 says "By faith we understand that the universe was formed at God's command, so that what is seen was not made out of what was visible." It takes faith to believe and accept there is a God, our Creator, and the Intelligent Designer, who made a way for salvation from sin through His Son Jesus Christ and teaches us how to live through His Holy Spirit. For believers, when we die and it turns out there is no God, we have lost nothing, and we will never know He wasn't waiting on the other side. For non-believers, when they die and it turns out there is an Almighty God, they have lost everything for infinity, perhaps tragically, eerily similar to the initial singularity posited by the Big Bang theory.... I'd rather all people accept and believe in our Creator.